Heaven is a far better place

HEAVEN

IS A FAR BETTER PLACE

What the Bible teaches about heaven

Eryl Davies

 EVANGELICAL PRESS

EVANGELICAL PRESS
Grange Close, Faverdale North Industrial Estate, Darlington, DL3
0PH, England

First published 1999

British Library Cataloguing in Publication Data available

ISBN 0 85234 423 6

Printed and bound in Great Britain by Creative Print & Design Wales, Ebbw Vale

To the glory of God
and in thanksgiving for
my father, parents-in-law and niece, Andrea Keddie,
who are now 'with the Lord'.
We miss them deeply.

Contents

Section IV: Heaven: its challenge

Preface

The background to this book is described in chapter 1, but it has been both a privilege and a considerable challenge to write on the subject of heaven. The privilege has been that of reflecting in depth on heaven and its glories over a five-year period. The challenge has been at least twofold.

The first was that of allocating time to the project alongside the demands of teaching and preaching. However, the publishers have shown patience and I am grateful to them for their encouragement to complete the manuscript. I also appreciated the detailed observations of their readers on many of the chapters.

A second challenge has been that of searching the Scriptures and wrestling with various texts and themes. The benefit to me has been immense, both in terms of understanding the subject better and in appreciating even more the glorious future awaiting all Christians. Some of my conclusions, however, are tentative, particularly with regard to degrees of rewards in heaven for Christians. My intention is not to be controversial, or critical of others, but rather to explore what the Scriptures actually teach.

My thanks are due to Mrs Chris Connor, who prepared and edited the text on disk throughout the period of preparation and relieved me of a great deal of tedious work. I am also indebted to my wife for her thorough proof-reading of the manuscript prior to publication.

What else can I say? I am only too aware of the defects in this book and of my own inability to understand fully or convey adequately to you the breathtaking beauty and indescribable glories as well as privileges of heaven. But through the Bible, and to a lesser extent the testimony of some godly Christians, I have caught a new, stimulating glimpse of heaven. I pray that the Lord will bless you similarly through this book.

May the triune God be honoured in the lives of all who read these pages.

Eryl Davies
Evangelical Theological College of Wales
Bryntirion, Bridgend
March 1999

Section I
Heaven: an introduction

1.
Heaven: a shock!

To say the least, it was a shock! A real shock too! Let me explain the circumstances to you. In October 1994 I was due to lecture in a major conference at the Korean Torch Centre for World Missions in Seoul on the themes of death, hell and heaven. I was the only scheduled speaker throughout the four-day conference and my task was to lecture a total of sixteen times, four times each day. It was a demanding and tiring schedule but extremely enjoyable and invigorating. And the conference members responded well to the ministry of the Word. However, the shock came several weeks before the conference started. The organizers planned to provide an attractive file including a summary of all my lectures to each conference member and for this reason they needed my outlines well in advance. By mid-July I had faxed a summary of my lectures on death and hell. I had researched and written on these subjects extensively, so there was no difficulty in providing a summary of those lectures. But what about heaven? Rather innocently, I explained to the conference organizers that I would fax an outline of my lectures on heaven 'within a few days'. After all, I thought, heaven would be easier to handle. That was in mid-July. A week later I was struggling with the subject of heaven. And it was a shock. I began to realize how little I understood and knew about the subject. There was an urgent need for me to search the Scriptures more thoroughly and to see what the Bible said about heaven. But it took time and the weeks passed by. I was surprised by the extensive biblical, especially New Testament, data on the subject, some of which is rich, stimulating and complex, raising all kinds of exegetical and hermeneutical as well as theological questions.

When I turned to read what the systematic theologians had written about heaven I had another shock and a major disappointment. Scant attention had been given to the subject by many of these respected theologians. For example, when I turned to Louis Berkhof's *Systematic Theology*[1] only one page out of 784 pages was devoted to the subject of heaven. And even that one page was hopelessly inadequate and superficial. Yes, I was shocked and my disappointment with Berkhof was repeated in the writings of several other systematic theologians. I understood the significance of Donald Guthrie's statement: 'It is not fashionable in theological thinking to attach too much importance to a study of the New Testament teaching on heaven.'[2] Sadly, I had to agree. But what about more general books on heaven? Again, I searched the library catalogues and was surprised to discover that only a small number of modern authors have written about heaven. Some of these books tend to be popular, brief, sometimes superficial and devotional. On the other hand, I was glad of the opportunity to read these books and at least to be reminded of heaven and challenged concerning it.

I am afraid it was late August before I was in a position to fax an outline of my lectures on heaven to the conference organizers in Seoul; my 'few days' had become a period of six weeks. But even after sending this outline, I knew I still had a considerable amount of thinking and research to do before the conference actually started.

And I am still studying the subject and reflecting on some aspects of heaven. It is a glorious subject; in fact, it is thrilling, exciting and challenging even to write about it. However, a note of warning is necessary at this point. This book is not intended as a definitive or exhaustive treatment of heaven; no, it is only an introduction. My main intention in writing the book is to share with you the fruits of my own study and thereby to stimulate you to think more about heaven and also to long for it, as well as to live here in the light of this glorious hope.

2.
Heaven on earth?

It had been a hard day at work. There was no time even to have a lunch-break. There were endless phone calls, interviews, complications with a client and, to make it worse, the car broke down on the way home. Over half an hour passed before an emergency rescue service arrived to repair the car and another twenty-five minutes before it was repaired. At last, the man reached home and he was relieved. After greeting his family and informing them of what had happened, he took off his jacket and shoes, then sat down in the nearest armchair. 'To sit here and relax', he muttered to his wife, 'is like heaven.' And he meant it, too.

Or the situation may be entirely different. Perhaps it is a holiday situation where a couple are relaxing in the country-side and enjoying a picnic on a warm, cloudless day. The scene is idyllic. Amid the trees and fields the only noise they hear is the singing of birds, the occasional bleating of sheep and the ripple of water from a nearby river. They both agree. It is 'heavenly' relaxing in such a beautiful and peaceful location.

For some young people the noun 'heaven' or the adjective 'heavenly' may be used after a period of intensive study and examinations either in school or university. Walking out of the final examination, they feel relieved it is all over and happy that at last they are able to relax and close their textbooks at least for some months, if not permanently. Yes, it is like 'heaven' to have finished their assessments. Alternatively, a patient may compare his feelings immediately after surgery, when he felt considerable pain and discomfort, with the comfort he later feels after making a complete recovery. His regained health and consequent happiness are described by him as being like 'heaven' and he is sincere in saying so.

We understand what people mean when they use words like 'heaven' or 'heavenly' in these contexts. They are referring to feelings of immense happiness, enjoyment, relief and satisfaction. According to this popular usage, heaven does not refer to a location and condition after death, but rather to an experience or attitude of contentment and happiness concerning one's circumstances in this present life.

Christians' use of the term

Christians, too, sometimes use the words 'heaven' or 'heavenly' to describe their enjoyment and experience of God in this present world. Samuel Rutherford, for example, was a famous Presbyterian minister in Scotland who died in 1661. After formal training, he was licensed as a preacher of the gospel in 1627 and became the minister of a small parish church in Anwoth in the area of Kirkcudbright. The tensions existing at that time between the English monarchs and many of the Presbyterians in Scotland concerning church government and religious liberty meant that many ordinary Christians, as well as ministers, were imprisoned and even martyred. Rutherford was one of the Covenanting ministers who refused to compromise his convictions to please the monarchy, so he was consequently exiled and imprisoned. During the period of his enforced exile in Aberdeen when he was forbidden to return to his church, he experienced in a deep way the glorious

presence and blessing of the Lord Jesus Christ. On 23 June
1637, for example, he wrote a letter from Aberdeen to Alexander Colvill. The letter was brief but revealing and challenging. One fact stands out in it: Rutherford was deeply in love
with Christ. He was captivated by the 'surpassing loveliness
of Christ'. And he longed to enjoy Christ more and more, not
only in glory but also here in this life. 'When Christ comes', he
wrote, 'he stays not long. But certainly the blowing of his
breath upon a poor soul is heaven upon earth...'[1]

Only a Christian can understand such words and longings.
The hymn-writer Bernard of Clairvaux expresses the point well:

> Jesus, the very thought of thee
> With sweetness fills my breast;
> But sweeter far thy face to see,
> And in thy presence rest.
> But what to those who find? Ah! This
> Nor tongue nor pen can show:
> The love of Jesus, what it is
> None but his loved ones know.

Until the miracle of new birth (John 3:3-8) takes place within
us, we are all strangers to God and separated from his fellowship. Even worse, due to our sinful nature we are God's enemies, rebelling against his authority and love. However, the
new birth changes us entirely. It is a supernatural, inward and
radical change which only the Lord can perform in our lives.
Afterwards, an intimate, spiritual union is divinely established
between each Christian and the Lord Jesus. Like Rutherford,
Christians want to know the reality and warmth of this relationship as well as to enjoy Christ's 'visits' to the soul.

This is often described as communion, or fellowship, with
God. And it is a reminder that Christianity involves more than
an intellectual assent to doctrines, or the living of a morally

good life. Truth is important, of course, as well as consistent behaviour, but at the heart of the Christian gospel is the offer of a personal, intimate relationship between the believer and the living, eternal God. It is an amazing fact. Ponder it for a moment. Because we are sinners, we have incurred God's anger and condemnation. This means we deserve eternal punishment in hell. But listen to the good news: God has taken the initiative in reconciling us to himself through the death of his Son, Jesus Christ. For those who believe on the Lord Jesus Christ, a right relationship with God is established and guaranteed. This is the basis of the sinner's friendship and communion with God.

Another example may help to illustrate the point further. Howell Harris was a Calvinistic Methodist exhorter in Wales during the eighteenth century. Not only was Harris greatly used by God but he also enjoyed deep experiences of God in revival. In his diary for 18 June 1735, for example, he records that in prayer he felt his heart 'suddenly … melting within … with love to God my Saviour…'. Such experiences of the Lord were neither unusual nor uncommon in his life. It was in 1739 that Harris used the term 'heaven' to describe such experiences of God. On this occasion he had met with the Rev. George Whitefield in Cardiff, South Wales. Whitefield, too, enjoyed a deep relationship with God and was greatly used as a preacher in England during the revival. The two men talked together in detail about their spiritual experiences. Reflecting later on their meeting, Harris reported, 'My soul was filled with heaven…'

Heaven on earth is the title of a book which was first published in 1654. The author, Thomas Brooks, was a Puritan pastor and he explains in the book how true Christians may fully experience assurance in their lives. The book is a classic; it is detailed, profound, but practical. Consider these words taken from his preface: 'To be in a state of true grace is to be miserable no more; it is to be happy for ever. A soul in this state is a soul near and dear to God… It is a soul housed in God … safe in everlasting arms… The being in a state of grace will yield a man a heaven hereafter, but the seeing of himself in this state will yield him both *a heaven here and a heaven here-after*; it will render him doubly blest, blest in heaven, and blest in his own conscience… To have grace, and to be sure that we have grace, is glory upon the throne, *it is heaven on this side of heaven*…'[2] (italics mine).

The use of the term 'heaven' by Christians like Rutherford, Harris and Brooks is clear. Without denying an objective location called heaven which awaits believers at death, they used the term on occasions in a more restricted way. For them, heaven was not the bliss of relaxing in an armchair at the end of a busy working day, nor was it the feeling of relief that examinations had finished. Again, heaven for them was vastly superior even to the enjoyment of picnicking in a beautiful location. These Christians had in mind something far more wonderful — namely, the enjoyment of Christ in our lives here and now. That was what Rutherford longed for and experienced. For Harris, it was not only his experience of Christ but also the rich time of talking about the Lord with Whitefield which led him to say that his soul was filled with heaven. Similarly, to know a deep assurance of being reconciled to God is 'heavenly' because of the pleasure, enjoyment and satisfaction it brings to an individual. And Brooks is not exaggerating. Such an assurance can be like heaven on this side of heaven.

What these Christian leaders claim is biblical, too. Heaven needs to be in the Christian before the Christian can be in heaven after death. Charles Spurgeon refers to an old Puritan Christian of whom it was said, 'Heaven was in him before he was in heaven.'[3] Spurgeon adds, 'That is necessary for all of us; we must have heaven in us before we get into heaven.' And he warned, 'If we do not get to heaven before we die, we shall never get there afterwards.' Spurgeon then relates the story of an old Scotsman who was asked whether he expected to go to heaven. His reply was firm and challenging: 'Man, I live there.' The Christian lives in heaven on earth. 'If men would go to heaven', wrote Jonathan Edwards, 'they must first be made fit for it.'[4] To be 'made fit' for heaven is to have our lives invaded by the God of heaven. He needs to place his Holy Spirit within us. By means of the miracle of new birth, our thoughts and affections are redirected towards God and heaven. The Christian is reorientated in his whole life. He is now heaven-bound and, in an important sense, heaven has already begun here with his newly found salvation and fellowship with the Lord.

Yes, our fellowship with God here is a foretaste of heaven itself. The new relationship with God enjoyed by Christians from conversion continues beyond death in heaven, but then it will be richer, perfect and visible. When dying, the Puritan John Preston was asked whether he was afraid. Although a mere whisper due to physical weakness, his answer was firm and joyous: 'No, I shall change my place, but I shall not change my company.'

While preaching on the words, 'Lay hold on eternal life' in 1 Timothy 6:12, Spurgeon urged Christians to 'often anticipate the joys of heaven'.[5] His exhortation continued, 'I think you and I do not go to heaven often enough.' Spurgeon then anticipated an objection: 'I thought we should go there when we died.' The reply of Spurgeon was in the affirmative: 'Yes, if you are a believer in Christ, that is secure; but why not go there now?' His point was a valid one. The position of the Christian here is unique, for he or she lives in two worlds at the same time. This continuity in our experience of God here and then later in heaven is essential. Heaven on earth for the Christian leads to heaven immediately at death.

The implications of this ugly word 'death' will be explored in the next two chapters.

3.
A fleeting shadow

Only after Christians die will they go to heaven. But 'death' is an ugly word. In fact, for many it can be a frightening word. For others, it has sad and painful associations. However, death is something which happens to us all in turn — friends, neighbours and relatives. One day even you will die. Perhaps you have not thought about it. Or it may be that you are so busy working or enjoying yourself that there is little time or desire to think about death or heaven. Well, you need to pause and think seriously about the subject. It is important for you to read on. Before we consider the significance of death in the next chapter, there is need first of all to underline the fact of the brevity and uncertainty of life in this world.

Life here is brief

At best, life on this earth for us is brief and temporary. We certainly do not stay here for ever. The brevity of human life is expressed in the Bible by Job:

> Man born of woman
>   is of few days and full of trouble.

> He springs up like a flower and withers away;
> like a fleeting shadow, he does not endure
>
> (Job 14:1-2).

The point is emphasized frequently in the Bible. For example, man's brief life is likened to grass and flowers:

> A voice says, 'Cry out.'
>   And I said, 'What shall I cry?'
> 'All men are like grass,
>   and all their glory is like the flowers of the field.
> The grass withers and the flowers fall,
>   because the breath of the LORD blows on them.
>   Surely the people are grass.
> The grass withers and the flowers fall,
>   but the word of our God stands for ever'
>   (Isa. 40:6-8; see also 1 Peter 1:24-25).

The comparison is a telling one. Only one thing is permanent and unchanging in this world. And that is God's Word. Everything else is transitory and brief.

The apostle James conveys the same message but in a different way. 'What is your life?' is his startling question. James wants us to think about the nature and length of our human lives. His answer is uncompromising and honest. 'You are a mist' (or, a puff of smoke), he insists, 'that appears for a little while and then vanishes' (James 4:14). It is a point well made. A life-span of seventy years can seem a very long time to us but it is only equivalent to approximately 25,500 days. If you are now thirty-five years old, and assuming you will live to reach the age of seventy, it means you only have about 13,000 days left. However, if you think that is a lot, remember that at least 4,000 out of the 13,000 days will be spent sleeping! Life is really like a mist or puff of smoke; it appears briefly and then disappears.

This fact of life's brevity filled Pascal, the French mathematician and philosopher, with fear and astonishment. 'When I consider the short duration of my life,' he wrote, 'swallowed up in the eternity before and after, the little space which I fill, and even can see, engulfed in the infinite immensity of space of which I am ignorant, and which knows me not, I am astonished being here rather than there, why now rather than then.'[1] There is no escape from the fact. For all of us, life at best is brief, 'a fleeting shadow'.

Life here is uncertain

Not only is life brief, it is also uncertain and unpredictable both in its length and quality. The evidence stares you in the face each day in one way or another. Possibly it is the shattering news of a young married couple whose baby has died in what is termed a 'cot-death'. Early in the evening the infant was healthy, smiling and contented. There was no indication at all that anything was likely to go wrong. Within six hours, however, the mother was shocked to find her baby motionless and dead in its cot. For others it may be a road accident in which a child is killed as it runs thoughtlessly on to a busy road. Or it may be a competent mountain climber who suddenly falls to his death.

Sometimes disease strikes our bodies and reminds us that we are vulnerable and weak. For example, an attractive fifteen-year-old girl died from cystic fibrosis, a cruel disease which strikes slowly but progressively at the lungs and pancreas. Even the medical team expected her to live another five years or so and, like the family, were taken by surprise. The same element of surprise was present when a colleague of mine in the Christian ministry died at the age of forty-one. There was little warning. He had suffered from a headache for several days and, on a journey we shared together, I saw him resting his head on the rear seat in the car. He was in considerable discomfort but he imagined it was a migraine. However, within three days he was rushed into hospital with a brain haemorrhage and died soon afterwards. His useful ministry as a preacher of the gospel had been cut short unexpectedly. Or I think of the tragic case of two children whose parents both died within a period of three years. One parent died suddenly in front of the children and the other parent died from cancer after a brief illness.

Such examples can be multiplied but the point is obvious. Human life, even at its best, is uncertain as well as brief. And we are fools if we do not prepare for life in the next world. Yes, fools. That is exactly what the Lord Jesus said on one occasion about a farmer whose only concern was to prosper, expand his business and enjoy himself. 'You fool!' were the words of God to him. 'This very night your life will be demanded from you' (Luke 12:20). It was unexpected as far as the farmer was concerned. However, he was short-sighted; his priorities were wrong and he was unprepared to die. In other words, he was a fool. What about you?

Life here can be incomplete

In one of his famous dialogues entitled *Georgias*, the famous Greek philosopher Plato likens human beings to jars which leak. Although one continues to fill the jar with water, it never remains full. It is a superb comparison. We fill our lives with various pleasures and ambitions, even work, yet we are never satisfied or complete. Our lives remain unfulfilled and, in a deep sense, empty. Some pleasures and experiences are enjoyable momentarily but later the sense of emptiness and lack of satisfaction and completeness can return with monotonous regularity.

Once again, the Bible underlines the point. The writer of Ecclesiastes, for example, provides a searching analysis of human life without God. Whether it is work, education or pleasure, he concludes that 'Everything is meaningless' (Eccles. 1:2). His analysis of pleasure is penetrating and challenging. 'What does pleasure accomplish?' is his question (2:2). He used wine to cheer himself and undertook all kinds of building projects in order to find a challenge and purpose in life. He became a multi-millionaire and hired servants as well as prostitutes to make himself happy. 'I denied myself nothing my eyes desired,' he reports. 'I refused my heart no pleasure' (2:10). And the result? Well, the writer paused to reflect on all his work, achievements and pleasure. His considered answer is given us in the next verse: 'Everything was meaningless, a chasing after the wind; nothing was gained under the sun' (2:11).

The main reason why humans experience a sense of emptiness and meaninglessness in their lives is the fact that they have been created in God's image. This means we all have an instinctive awareness of right and wrong and have been created to know, enjoy and glorify God. And it includes a longing for God even though we may not be able to recognize and articulate it. Without God, there is a void in our lives here and now. The world cannot satisfy us or give fulfilment. Augustine expressed the fact helpfully. Referring to God, he declared, 'You have made us for yourself, and our hearts are restless until they rest in you.'[2] C. S. Lewis affirms the same truth in his writing — namely, that humans have a longing, a desire, a deep and sometimes intense feeling which this world cannot satisfy. Lewis refers to 'a desire which no natural happiness will satisfy ... a desire, still wandering and uncertain of its object and still largely unable to see that object in the direction where it really lies'.[3]

This was my own experience as a teenager. With a happy, loving family life, everything seemed to be going for me. A secure job, higher education opening up before me and the prospect of gaining university degrees and a better job — what more did I need? I was good at sport, enjoyed music, even went to church and I had a girlfriend, too. But... Yes, something was missing. There was a gap; at times, it felt like a big hole in my life. I was groping and searching; sometimes the restlessness within was painful and dark. I needed God, but so do you. In the next chapter, we move forward to consider that ugly word 'death'.

4.
Death and all that

It is that word again — death. But there is no point in trying to evade it. As we have seen, life here is brief and uncertain. One day we shall all die. 'Man is destined to die once...' (Heb. 9:27), the Bible confirms. 'Death came to all...' (Rom. 5:12). Secular authors like Max Scheler agree: 'It is of the essence of everyone's experience of life, and of our own, that our lives are directed towards death.'[1]

In this chapter the plan is to look briefly at the fact and significance of death. Did you know, for example, that the term 'death' has more than one meaning in the Bible? It will be helpful, therefore, to explore the subject further and establish what the Bible actually teaches on the subject.

Physical death

Physical death is a stark reality, yet it is not easy defining and deciding when a person has died physically. An obvious answer is to say that a person is dead when he no longer breathes and his heart stops beating, but sometimes, as a result of significant advances in medical science, the question can be more complex. A person may be kept 'alive' artificially in hospital by means of a life-support machine. The patient's brain may have been damaged beyond recall yet other organs in the body are maintained by the machine. Brain-stem death leads to irreversible coma and medics usually regard this as a satisfactory criterion of brain death. The life-support machine is then switched off as the patient is regarded as 'dead' in any meaningful sense of the term. However, death is more easily recognized in the majority of cases.

How has physical death entered the world? The Bible tells us that death did not come about by chance. Far from it. God himself rightly introduced death as a punishment on man for his rebellion and disobedience. Think about it. Crime, dishonesty, violence, greed, immorality and terrorism continue to characterize human life and behaviour. What is the reason for such evils? Why is there so much misery in the world? The answer is found in the Bible. In the beginning God created a perfect world. The first two humans, Adam and Eve, were obedient (Gen. 1:27). They did not lie, steal, lose their temper nor behave selfishly or viciously. That is how God made our first parents. Unlike ourselves, they also knew God intimately and enjoyed pleasing and obeying him. Tragically, it all changed. And it happened suddenly. How? 'Sin', the Bible announces, 'entered the world through one man...' (Rom. 5:12). Here are seven crucial words which provide the answer to our question. One important point is that sin has not always been in the world. However, 'Sin entered the world'; a perfect, happy world created by God was suddenly spoilt when Adam and Eve disobeyed God.

Genesis chapter 3 informs us how this happened. Commanded by God not to eat the fruit of a particular tree (Gen. 2:16-17), the couple listened to the devil's lies and suggestions, then disobeyed the divine command (Gen. 3:1-6). The result was disastrous. Through their disobedience, sin invaded and affected thereafter the entire human race. There was more. As promised, God punished our first parents. Pain for women

in child-birth, toil and sweat in cultivating the land now cursed
with weeds, disease and disharmony were some of the punish-
ments imposed by God on them and on ourselves (vv. 16-19).
That was not the end either. 'For dust you are', God told Adam,
'and to dust you will return' (v. 19). Here is the significance of
the statement in Romans 5:12: 'Sin entered the world through
one man, and death through sin…' If there had been no sin,
there would not have been death, for 'The wages of sin is
death' (Rom. 6:23). Do not blame God for all the suffering
and wickedness in the world. Man, not God, has spoilt creation and rebelled against the good, yet holy God. Physical
death has come as a result of human sin.

Spiritual death

I can imagine the reaction of some readers to this sub-title.
'What on earth does this mean?' they may ask or, 'What is the
difference, if any, between spiritual and physical death?' The
questions are honest and appropriate, so let me begin my
answer by referring to an important statement in the Bible:
'As for you, you were dead in your transgressions and sins'
(Eph. 2:1). Admittedly, the apostle Paul is writing to Christians, but he is referring here to their pre-Christian lives which
were characterized by spiritual death.

   That was what I used to be like — a decent, religious and
sporty teenager yet, as far as God was concerned, unresponsive and dead. Allow me to illustrate the point. I remember a
young Christian visiting my room in college regularly in order
to tell me about the gospel. He talked about sin, a holy God,
God's Son dying for our sin as our substitute, the necessity for
me to repent and trust personally in the Lord Jesus Christ alone
for salvation. His witness was biblical, regular and consistent.

In fact, he was persistent and did not leave me alone for months. I was impressed by the quality of his life but I could not understand what he was saying. It did not make sense to me and I had no interest in the gospel. I was blind, unconcerned and unresponsive. That is spiritual death and my friend even despaired of my becoming a Christian.

At the same time, as I relaxed on the university campus, I sometimes observed Christian students going to their lunchtime meetings. In my opinion, they were unnatural and otherworldly; they gave me the creeps! And I wanted nothing to do with them. I hated what they represented and their faith seemed foolish to me. Again that is spiritual death. A lack of interest in God, a rejection of the gospel message, with its accompanying blindness, hostility and preference for sin, constitutes spiritual death.

The Bible provides much better examples. Saul of Tarsus was a thoroughly respectable and religious man. He was steeped in Jewish religion. His knowledge of the Old Testament Scripture was thorough; as a specialist teacher of God's Word he was automatically a member of the Jewish parliament. Nevertheless, he was spiritually dead and blind. Saul had no time for Christ. He hated the gospel and thought it was his duty to destroy Christianity by imprisoning and killing Christians. Saul's name struck terror into the hearts of Christians. There was no spiritual life in Saul's heart and no positive response to the gospel. Spiritual death characterized him.

Before such people can enter heaven, they need to be changed from within. The answer is new birth and conversion. This involves a radical, transforming and supernatural work that only God can do within us. Without this, we cannot go to heaven. And that is what Jesus Christ emphasized: 'I tell you the truth, no one can see the kingdom of God unless he is born again… Flesh gives birth to flesh, but the Spirit gives birth to spirit. You should not be surprised at my saying, "You must be born again" ' (John 3:3,6-7). Without this spiritual rebirth, heaven would be a terror and certainly not a delight.

Eternal death

A third use of the term 'death' in the Bible relates to eternal death, which is the eternal punishment of unbelievers in hell[2] after death. Like 'heaven', the term 'hell' is used on occasions to describe experiences in this life, but experiences which are distressing and painful rather than happy and enjoyable. Famine conditions, an earthquake, war, terminal illness, drugs, a broken marriage, rape and injustice can be 'hellish' experiences for the victims. Hell, many claim, only refers to these painful, harsh conditions and experiences in our present lives. Some also argue that you make your own hell on earth. Those who flout Bible guidelines concerning sex and marriage, for example, are more likely to become infected with the deadly AIDS virus. The use of drugs and glue-sniffing as a child can lead to intolerable suffering, addiction, and even death, in teenage years. A person who smokes cigarettes is more likely to die of lung cancer or heart disease. But is this all the word 'hell' means? Or is there, in addition, a hell beyond this life?

Once again we turn to the Bible for our answer. Obviously we are responsible for our behaviour and 'A man reaps what he sows' (Gal. 6:7). While we can reap some of the consequences of our behaviour in this life, that is not the whole story. The Bible tells us that hell is a real place and condition to which unbelievers go when they die. This is what Jesus Christ referred to when he warned his disciples, 'Do not be afraid of those who kill the body but cannot kill the soul. Rather, be afraid of the one [God] who can destroy both soul and body in hell' (Matt. 10:28).

On another occasion the Lord Jesus related the story of the rich man and Lazarus (Luke 16:19-31). The latter was desperately poor and begged for his daily food, while the former lived in the lap of luxury. Eventually both men died and the Lord tells us what happened to them. Lazarus, because he trusted in God, went to heaven (v. 22). By contrast, because the rich man was not a believer he went immediately to 'hell' (the Greek word is *Hades*) when he died. Our Lord makes it clear that hell is a place of unimaginable suffering and agony for unbelievers beyond death (vv. 23-28).

Furthermore, the Lord Jesus spoke of those who would be 'thrown outside, into the darkness, where there will be weeping and gnashing of teeth' (Matt. 8:12). Unbelievers will hear the awful sentence from the Judge: 'Depart from me, you who are cursed, into the eternal fire prepared for the devil and his angels' (Matt. 25:41). These are all references to a real place which the Bible calls hell.

Unless we have been rescued personally by Christ, we are all on this road to hell. We are in great danger. Heaven is not for all.

5.
Who goes to heaven?

Undoubtedly this is a question of major importance. Who goes to heaven? This question relates to the identity and qualifications of those who go to heaven when they die. The consistent Bible answer to the question is uncompromising: only Christians can go to heaven. You may not agree, or may want to modify the answer somewhat. Possibly you think that everyone should go to heaven, irrespective of their religion or behaviour. But I challenge your opinion, for the Bible must be the absolute standard for deciding what we believe or do. After all, the Bible is God's Word; here alone we read of what God has said and done.

Consider, then, some of the words of Jesus Christ on the subject. He spoke about two roads, two classes of people and two different destinations. Concluding his famous Sermon on the Mount, Christ emphasizes the fact that 'Wide is the gate and broad is the road that leads to destruction, and many enter through it. But small is the gate and narrow the road that leads to life, and only a few find it' (Matt. 7:13-14). On another occasion, he reassures us that 'Whoever believes in him is not condemned,' but then he goes on to warn: 'But whoever does not believe stands condemned already because he has not believed in the name of God's one and only Son' (John 3:18). There are two groups of people, believers and unbelievers, but in addition there are also two different destinations after death — heaven and hell. This will become clearer in this chapter as we describe the characteristics of those who go to heaven. For example, what is different about Christians? How are they qualified to enter heaven while others are refused entrance? To enter heaven, the Bible insists that we must be rescued, reconciled, reborn, received and refashioned. These requirements will now be explained in more detail in this chapter and the next.

We must be rescued

The concept of rescue is familiar to us all. Perhaps it is a child struggling in the sea as the current takes her further away from the shore. A lifeguard is alerted to the danger and he swims out and reaches the frightened child. She has been rescued and brought to safety. Or it may be a climber who falls dangerously down part of the rocks. He is unable to walk and lies on an inaccessible and dangerous ledge. Colleagues and onlookers have no choice but to call the emergency services. Within minutes, a rescue helicopter arrives and the injured man is winched slowly into the helicopter and taken to hospital. The rescue is completed. Similar rescues occur all the time in one way or another and people are rescued from danger, even imminent death.

It is this concept of rescue which underlines much of what the Bible says about the death of the Lord Jesus Christ. He died in order to rescue us. Hopelessly unable as we were to rescue ourselves from the power and punishment of our own sin, 'Christ died for the ungodly... God demonstrates his own love for us in this: While we were still sinners, Christ died for us' (Rom. 5:6,8). One Greek word for 'rescue' is used in Galatians 1:4 to describe the purpose of Christ's sacrifice of himself on the cross: 'who gave himself for our sins to rescue us…' The word implies great danger, as well as the inability of the people concerned to escape from the danger by their own efforts. On the cross, therefore, the Lord Jesus achieved a special rescue operation. The same idea of rescue occurs again in 1 Thessalonians 1:10: '… Jesus, who rescues us from the coming wrath'. Only those who trust personally in Jesus Christ are rescued from God's anger, but notice that it is the Lord Jesus *alone* who is able to rescue us from this 'coming wrath'.

A key word in this context is 'propitiation' which is used in the Authorized Version of the Bible in at least two major statements: 'Whom God hath set forth to be a propitiation through faith in his blood, to declare his righteousness for the remission of sins that are past' (Rom. 3:25); and 'Herein is love, not that we loved God, but that he loved us, and sent his Son to be the propitiation for our sins' (1 John 4:10). The word 'propitiation' tells us something extremely important about the sacrifice of Jesus Christ. 'To propitiate' means to turn away and divert anger by means of a sacrifice. And that is what the Lord Jesus did when he died for us on the cross. A major diversion took place there. The tidal wave of God's wrath that was due to us fell instead on the Lord Jesus. He was made sin for us and really rescued us.

We must be reconciled

It is possible to rescue an enemy or a person we do not like from danger but without becoming friends with that person. During the Second World War, for example, enemy personnel who jumped into the sea from a bombed and sinking ship or submarine would sometimes be rescued by an Allied ship and taken back as war prisoners. Despite the rescue, they were kept in a prisoner-of-war camp for the duration of the war and treated as enemies.

Now God's dealings with those who believe in Jesus Christ are different. The word 'reconciliation' assumes that a broken relationship between two persons has been repaired; these two persons, previously enemies, now become genuine friends. Consider this in regard to our relationship with God.

Ever since the major disaster of Adam and Eve, alienation and enmity have been the most prominent features of this broken relationship between God and man. This alienation is expressed in two ways. First of all, from our side there is hostility towards God. We are opposed to God in our hearts. When his law conflicts with our own desires then we instinctively go our own way, not God's. Our instinctive bias is against God. Notice how this fact is repeatedly stated in the Bible: 'We were God's enemies' (Rom. 5:10). 'The sinful mind is hostile to God. It does not submit to God's law, nor can it do so' (Rom. 8:7). 'The man without the Spirit does not accept the things that come from the Spirit of God, for they are foolishness to him, and he cannot understand them' (1 Cor. 2:14). 'Once you were alienated from God and were enemies in your minds' (Col. 1:21).

The cause of our hostility and bias is sin. But that is only one side of the problem. In fact, the other side of the problem is much more serious. God is alienated from us. He is against us. And we are told the reason for this: it is because God is holy and he is angry with us because of our sin. He is against us because of our sin (Ps. 1:4-6; 5:4-6; 37:38). Sin arouses God's hostility and the wrath of God is a reality we dare not ignore (Rom.1:18; 2:5-8; 5:9-10; 1 Thess. 1:10; 2:16).

Reconciliation, therefore, is the answer to this major problem of enmity and alienation between God and man. The enmity of God towards us is removed only by the unique sacrifice of Jesus Christ. He removed the hostility of God by taking the guilt and punishment of our sin upon himself. Three basic facts concerning reconciliation need to be understood at this point. First, *it is entirely the work of God.* He devised and accomplished it; there is no contribution on our part. 'God was reconciling the world to himself...' (2 Cor. 5:19). Second, as we have seen, *this reconciliation was achieved by God 'through the death of his Son'* (Rom. 5:10). Jesus Christ took our place by suffering the punishment that was due to us. Third, *this reconciliation was completed and obtained once for all at Calvary* when Jesus Christ died in the place of sinners. It really is good news. Sinners like ourselves can be reconciled to a holy God and become his friends, even his children.

We must be reborn

Picture a river when it is completely frozen up in winter. Nothing is able to move in the river and even boats have to anchor in port for many weeks. When spring arrives and the thaw sets in, the ice begins to break up and the flow of water can be observed once again. Despite the thaw, however, large pieces of ice are still present in the river for a few weeks. Eventually, in the warmer weather, all traces of ice and snow disappear. Now the river flows normally and ships as well as smaller boats can use it for pleasure and business.

I want to use this picture to illustrate what God does in preparing us to become Christians. The frozen river points to the person who is not a Christian. His heart is frozen towards God and there is no flow of love, obedience or worship to God in his life. He is in the grip of sin; blind, wilful, rebellious and selfish. In fact, he is a slave to sin. It is in this dreadful condition that God works a miracle in his or her life. And it is a miracle — a radical, supernatural, inward and life-transform-ing work. The Bible describes it as being 'born again'. The

Lord Jesus Christ talked about it and insisted that no one can become a Christian or enter heaven without being born again. 'No one can see the kingdom of God,' he warns, 'unless he is born again' (John 3:3). Later, the Lord Jesus emphasizes the necessity of the new birth: 'Flesh gives birth to flesh, but the Spirit gives birth to spirit' (v. 6). In other words, a sinful human nature cannot make itself spiritual and clean. That is impossible for us to do. Left to ourselves we would never desire or love God. While man is capable of outstanding scientific, engineering and medical achievements, yet he cannot give spiritual life to himself or to others. Only God can do that. And God does it by the Holy Spirit who puts spiritual life into our dead hearts so that we are born again. Consequently, we have new desires, new values, new standards, new aims and new pleasures. We have become a new creation (Eph. 2:10; 2 Cor. 5:17) and have passed from death to life.

To return to our river illustration, the thawing of the frozen river can be likened to the new birth when the Holy Spirit breaks the power and grip of sin in our lives. No longer are we slaves to sin (see, for example, Rom. 6:11-18) and we are free to move towards God regularly in love and obedience. To enter heaven, therefore, it is essential to be reborn. Let me put it in another way and more positively. Heaven is full only of people who have been rescued, reconciled and reborn. In the next chapter we will look at further requirements for those who go to heaven.

6.
Heaven: entrance requirements

As we have already seen, we must be *rescued* — from sin and the punishment of hell we rightly deserve. Consequently, heaven is populated only by sinners who have been rescued by the Lord. We must be *reconciled* — to a holy God whom we have wronged and angered. There can be no heaven without reconciliation, for otherwise God will remain our enemy. We must be *reborn* — changed inwardly and miraculously by the Holy Spirit and made new persons. It is this rebirth which enables us to love and obey God, who is himself the supreme attraction of heaven. No wonder, then, that Christians in heaven are thrilled and in ecstasy over God's kindness and grace to them.

Now in this chapter we draw attention to two further necessary requirements for entrance into heaven, namely, that we must receive Christ and be redirected.

We must receive Christ

Jesus Christ died on the cross to rescue sinners; this is a historical fact. To put it differently and in more theological terms, reconciliation between rebellious, condemned sinners and a holy God has been achieved for us by God himself in his Son, the Lord Jesus. Here is the good news of the gospel. And it really is marvellous news. But what was achieved for us by Christ needs to be accepted and received personally by each person. Even though forgiveness and salvation have been fully paid for by Jesus Christ, a response is needed on our part to what God has done. This response, or receiving, is known as conversion, which in turn comprises two integral elements, repentance and faith.

1. Repentance

'Repentance' may be a big word, but it is a key word. All it means is that a person turns away from sin and turns to God in obedience. Some basic knowledge is involved: for example, knowledge about God, his holy character and his perfect law which we are obliged to keep; knowledge, too, about ourselves, that we have failed hopelessly to obey and please God. However, repentance involves more than knowledge; there is also an element of conviction, distress, concern and anxiety because of our wrong relationship to God. But there is even more. Repentance is a gift and involves forsaking particular sins and also a life of sin; it means turning in a radically different direction, from disobedience and sin, to God and obedience. This was the message of the Lord Jesus Christ when he went 'proclaiming the good news of God. "The time has come," he said. "The kingdom of God is near. Repent and believe the good news!" ' (Mark 1:14-15). The apostles preached the same message: 'Repent ... every one of you, in the name of Jesus Christ for the forgiveness of your sins...' (Acts 2:38; cf. 3:19; 17:30).

2. Faith

Faith or, to be more precise, saving faith, is also a gift and is inseparably related to repentance. Theologians have often asked which of these two elements, repentance or faith, comes first. But you cannot have one without the other. The faith that trusts in Christ for salvation is a repenting faith, while real repentance is a believing repentance. They must go together.

What then is faith? The crowning element of faith is our receiving and resting upon Christ for salvation. It is not merely believing or feeling things about God or Christ, however true and profound they may be. Faith involves trusting a person, the person of the Lord Jesus, the one alone who saves sinners. To put it in a different but equally biblical way, faith involves receiving Christ. Notice how this is emphasized in John 1:12: 'Yet to all who received him, to those who believed in his name, he gave the right to become children of God...' In other words, believing involves receiving Christ. Later in the New Testament the same principle is stressed: 'Just as you received Christ Jesus as Lord, continue to live in him...' (Col. 2:6).

While listening to a brief sermon on the words, 'Look unto me, and be ye saved, all the ends of the earth' (Isa. 45:22, AV), the teenager Charles Spurgeon was challenged directly by the preacher to 'look to Jesus Christ'. 'Look! Look!' he was told. 'You have nothing to do but look and live!' For Spurgeon it was a special moment and he tells us what happened: 'I saw at once the way of salvation and I looked until I could have looked my eyes away... I came to Christ, my soul cast itself on Jesus... I found the Saviour.' Now, at last, Spurgeon had received and trusted Christ. In other words, he became a real Christian. Or, we can say that Calvary was then personalized for the teenager. What about you? Remember that only those who have received Christ enter heaven.

We must be redirected

I was in a hurry and there was hardly any time to spare. I had to attend an important meeting and it was due to commence within forty minutes at a venue about twenty miles away. Seated comfortably in my car, I was driving along the motorway on the way to my meeting. And then it happened. In the distance I saw police cars flashing their blue lights and the traffic ahead had come to a halt. Within seconds, I too was stationary in a long traffic queue. You guessed right. There was a major accident ahead. Within minutes, however, a policeman indicated that some cars, including my own, could proceed a little further by driving along the hard shoulder in order to take an exit road. The policeman reassured us that we would then be redirected and given an alternative route. It worked, too. At strategic points, police personnel redirected our cars and we found ourselves travelling by a radically different route.

In a sense, this is what happens to those who become Christians: they are redirected. Becoming a Christian through receiving Christ and his salvation can happen in all kinds of circumstances — quietly, privately or gradually, or more dramatically and suddenly. Sometimes God uses emergencies on the road of life to stop us in our aimless, selfish and sinful behaviour. An illness, the death of a near relative, the loss of a job, financial or marital problems can all make us stop and think about ourselves and God and the future. Perhaps God is using similar circumstances at present to bring you to Christ. If so, I encourage you to respond by trusting and receiving the Lord Jesus Christ as your personal Saviour. Having received Christ, you find that he redirects your life. Yes, the new birth makes you a new person and you need to live in obedience to God. Such obedience is the fruit and outworking of the Holy Spirit who indwells all Christians. There is need for Christians to struggle and fight against sin and to persevere in obedience and trust; their lives have been redirected. And only such people go to heaven; for 'Without holiness no one will see the Lord' (Heb. 12:14).

Section II
Heaven: some basic information

7.
Heaven: what it really means

As we saw in chapter 2, the term 'heaven' is often used to refer to very different kinds of experiences and situations. The word has been stretched like elastic in order to include several contrasting ideas or experiences. There is an urgent need to be more precise and accurate in its use. But this also raises questions. For example, what is the original and proper meaning of the term 'heaven'? This in turn involves a prior question: how is the word 'heaven' understood and used in the Bible? Although such a question is foundational, some readers may object and ask why we are referring at all to the Bible. What is special about the Bible? This last question is fair and we need to answer it immediately, even if only briefly.

What is special about the Bible?

The Bible consists of sixty-six individual books. Varying in length and style, these sixty-six books were originally written either in Hebrew, Aramaic or Greek by approximately forty writers over a period of 1700 years. That in itself indicates that the Bible is a remarkable book. These forty writers, however, were not expressing their own ideas. Far from it. What happened was that they spoke and wrote accurately what God had given them: 'All Scripture is God-breathed...' (2 Tim. 3:16). To put it another way, the Bible originates with God, not with humans. The writers were God's spokesmen; they thought and wrote what, on occasions, God revealed to them. The Bible, therefore, is God's book. And it is important, therefore, to know and believe what the Bible says.

Another fact concerning the Bible should be noted, namely, that it is reliable. The author is the 'God who does not lie' (Titus 1:2). God does not say anything in the Bible which is untrue. His book can be trusted. Remember, too, that a great deal of the Bible's teaching and many of its predictions have already been fulfilled. God means what he says and it is certain to take place. Because the Bible is reliable and tells us about God, his plans and the future, it is essential that we refer to it and believe what it says. We are fools if we ignore the Bible. For example, if patients ignore the directions of a competent medical consultant then they are acting irresponsibly. Similarly, a motorist who ignores the laws relating to driving a car on a public highway is being extremely foolish. In both cases, the consequences could be disastrous. By contrast, the Bible is even more important. This is God's book. It is the only book in which God has chosen to give us answers to our ultimate questions. We have no choice in these pages, then, but to refer often to the Bible. Anyway, it is the Bible which originally and exclusively tells us about heaven. This is our primary textbook for reliable information concerning heaven.

What does the term 'heaven' refer to?

We can now proceed with our main theme. The question we are asking in this chapter concerns the meaning of the word 'heaven' in the Bible. What does 'heaven' refer to? And we now have some homework to do.

In the Hebrew Old Testament, *samayim* is the word most frequently used for heaven; it means 'the heights' or 'upper regions'. Other Hebrew words, like *shackaq*, mean 'clouds' and 'sky'. The New Testament Greek equivalent is *ouranos*, which has a similar meaning of being 'raised up'. James Packer claims that in both the Old and New Testaments heaven literally means 'sky'.[1] The primary meaning of all the original words used in the Bible for heaven is 'that which is above';[2] it refers to what is above the earth or above man. This idea of what is above implies the 'ethical concept of something high, as against that which is low, something noble rather than common, something of a celestial nature rather than terrestrial or earthy'.[3]

Different meanings

What is important to notice here is that these Hebrew and Greek words translated as 'heaven' are used in different ways and with different meanings in the Bible. For example, the very first verse in the Bible is helpful at this point: 'In the beginning God created the heavens and the earth' (Gen. 1:1). The term 'heavens' in this statement is in the plural and the combined reference to 'the heavens and the earth' emphasizes that the entire universe — that is, the earth, space and other planets — was created by God. Later, in the same chapter, the word is used in verse 17 to refer to the wider expanse of space in which the sun, moon and other planets are located, and it is interesting to compare the Authorized Version (AV) and the New International Version (NIV) translations of this verse. According to the AV, God set the sun, moon and other planets 'in the firmament of the heaven', while the NIV translates it as 'the expanse of the sky'.

Astronomers remind us of the vastness of space, referring to the stratosphere (20-30 miles high), the mesosphere (30-50 miles), the ionosphere (50-300 miles) and the exosphere (80-100 miles), which then merges into interplanetary space. On 20 July 1969 man set foot for the first time on the moon when Apollo 11's commander, Neil Armstrong, stepped off the ladder of the lunar module. TV viewers worldwide heard his first words: 'That's one small step for man, one giant leap for mankind.' It took four days after lift-off to put Armstrong on the moon, about 190,000 miles away. However, the nearest star to our solar system, Proxima Centauri, is three and a half light years away — seventeen million, million miles. This vast expanse is occasionally referred to in the Bible as the 'heavens'. But the word can also refer to the skies which are immediately visible above us and where the birds fly (see, for example, Gen. 1:20).

God's dwelling-place

However, the term 'heaven' is used primarily in the Bible to refer to God's dwelling-place. This is the sense in which it is used by the Lord Jesus in the opening words of what we call the Lord's Prayer: 'Our Father in heaven...' (Matt. 6:9). The Old Testament confirms this fact:

> From heaven the LORD looks down
>   and sees all mankind;
> from his dwelling-place he watches
>   all who live on earth...

> (Ps. 33:13-14).

Or, consider the prayer of the prophet Isaiah, who pleads with God to 'Look down from heaven and see from your lofty throne, holy and glorious'(Isa. 63:15). Later, we read, 'This is what the Lord says: "Heaven is my throne and the earth is my footstool" ' (Isa. 66:1).

Heaven is where God is. It is not surprising that the God whose home is heaven is also described as the 'God of heaven' (2 Chron. 36:23; Neh. 1:5; Ps. 136:26). From heaven also the Lord Jesus Christ came into this world. On several occasions the Lord Jesus emphasized this fact. Referring to himself, he declared, 'For the bread of God is he who comes down from heaven and gives life to the world' (John 6:33). He added, 'For I have come down from heaven...' (v. 38). Do not miss this important point. Heaven is also the home of Christ. Before his incarnation, the Lord Jesus, as of right, was in heaven with the Father. In this context, one further point needs to be emphasized.

Heaven is a place

Heaven is a place, not merely a condition or experience. Some evangelical writers, however, are reluctant to affirm the fact. Millard Erickson, for example, insists that heaven 'is primarily a state'.[4] Donald Guthrie, too, reasons that 'We shall not expect, however, to find a description of a place, so much as the presence of a person.'[5] He later expresses the opinion that 'Paul does not think of heaven as a place, but thinks of it in terms of the presence of God.'[6] I understand what Guthrie is attempting to say. It is true, for example, that the Bible does not provide us with a detailed description of heaven's location. After all, the glory of heaven is not so much the place, but the presence of the living God who dwells there. Paul longed to see and be with the Lord in heaven, but it was the Lord, not the place so much, which attracted the apostle. This focus on God is correct. One fears, however, that writers like Erickson and Guthrie do not give sufficient weight to the fact that heaven is, nevertheless, a place. A. A. Hodge maintains a good balance in maintaining that heaven is both 'a definite place' and 'a state of blessedness'.[7] And he is correct. 'To think of heaven as a place', writes James Packer, 'is more right than wrong', for it 'appears in Scripture as a spatial reality...'[8] although invisible to us here. The 'closeness to us of heaven', however, is for Packer 'a matter of solid spiritual fact'.

There are good reasons for insisting that heaven is a place. Consider a few of these reasons briefly. The risen Christ, for example, ascended to heaven. Yes, it was a shock for the disciples. One moment he was answering their questions and speaking about the Holy Spirit. But the next moment Jesus was 'taken up before their very eyes, and a cloud hid him from their sight' (Acts 1:9). It was completely unexpected on their part. And they were shocked. All they could do was to keep on 'looking intently up into the sky as he was going' (v. 10). Suddenly, two angels stood by them and spoke: '... This same Jesus, who has been taken from you into heaven, will come back in the same way you have seen him go into heaven' (v. 11). Notice the emphasis on heaven. 'It is hard', writes Grudem, 'to imagine how the fact of Jesus' ascension to a place could be taught more clearly.'[9]

Or think of the way Stephen was stoned to death by his religious enemies. Before he died, he 'looked up to heaven and saw the glory of God, and Jesus standing at the right hand of God' (Acts 7:55). It must have been a glorious sight. And Stephen had to tell people about it. ' "Look", he said, "I see heaven open and the Son of Man standing at the right hand of God" ' (v. 56). Within minutes of seeing the glorified Christ, Stephen himself would have entered heaven. Remember, too, the promise of Jesus to all believers: 'I am going there to prepare a place for you' (John 14:2). And he is referring to heaven as a place: '... that you also may be where I am' (v. 3). At the Second Coming of the Lord Jesus, believers will receive a resurrection body like that of Christ and we shall enter heaven glorified (see 1 Cor. 15:50-57; Phil. 3:21). There is no doubt about it. Heaven is a place. In the next chapter we need to discuss the matter further and ask, where is this place called heaven?

8.
Heaven: where it is

In the previous chapter we established several important points concerning heaven. We indicated the variety of ways in which the Hebrew and Greek words translated as 'heaven' in the Bible are also used deliberately to refer either to the universe, the wider expanse of space, or to the skies immediately above us. The most important meaning of the term 'heaven' in the Bible, however, is that of God's dwelling-place. Heaven is where God is. This point is extremely important and it will be necessary for us to grapple with its significance in more detail in the next chapters.

As we have seen, heaven is a definite place, although the Bible does not satisfy our curiosity and inform us where it is. Interestingly, neither the Lord Jesus nor the apostles in the New Testament provide us with details concerning the location of heaven. Here is a warning for us to refrain from merely speculating where heaven might be. More important is the fact that heaven is where God is.

It can be helpful to pause here in order to discuss in a little more detail heaven's location and, at the same time, anticipate an important question.

For example, does not the Bible use expressions like 'up' and 'above' to describe heaven? Yes, it does and such expressions as 'up' and 'above' are used in several Bible references to heaven. Here are just a few examples. Referring to his home in heaven, the Lord Jesus declared, 'I am from above' (John 8:23). Notice how he describes heaven here as being 'above'. Our Lord then strengthens the point by contrasting himself with his hearers: 'You are from below... You are of this world; I am not of this world.' Jesus Christ and his hearers belonged essentially to two realms;[1] in this respect, there was an 'infinite chasm'[2] between their respective origins, realms and values. Among other things, the Lord Jesus emphasizes his own pre-existence in this statement and also the fact that heaven is where he originates from; it is the place to which he belongs as of right. Earlier, he had used similar language in describing himself as 'the bread that came down from heaven' (John 6:41). Again, observe the terminology used: he 'came down' out of heaven and he alone is the one who is the real bread by giving and sustaining spiritual life in this world.

Again, in his ascension we are told that Jesus was 'taken up' into heaven (Luke 24:51). At the time of his personal return in glory to this world at the end of history, we are informed that the Lord will 'come down from heaven...' (1 Thess. 4:16). These are only a few examples chosen in order to illustrate how expressions like 'above', 'taken up' and 'come down' are used in the Bible with regard to heaven.

Critics

Sometimes critics of the Bible have laughed at such expressions and dismissed them as being pre-scientific, misleading and 'crudely spatial'.[3] Hymn-writers, too, like Albert Midlane have been criticized for using this kind of literal, spatial language to describe heaven:

>   There's a home for little children
>   Above the bright blue sky.

One thing is clear. Heaven is not literally or spatially located just above the skies.

Two observations are appropriate here. First of all, expressions like 'up' and 'above' are metaphorical when used to refer to the location of heaven. This means that these descriptive terms are functioning in a particular way and are 'not literally applicable'[4] to heaven. They are picture words. Remember that the limitations of language become glaringly evident when we struggle to express what is other-worldly. Secondly, these descriptive terms used with regard to heaven are nevertheless useful and important. For example, they emphasize the fact of distance as well as difference between heaven and earth. Heaven is qualitatively different from our cosmos in that it is a spiritual, not a physical, location; heaven must never be regarded as a part or extension of this world. Behind these descriptive terms, then, is a message. Heaven is not accessible or observable to the naked eye. Nor is heaven a part of space, or subject to time. While heaven is a definite place, yet it is a spiritual one, other-worldly and radically different. The Bible does not allow us to be more specific than this concerning the location of heaven.

It is significant that the Lord Jesus himself never talked to his disciples concerning the location of heaven. Although he is God and had lived in heaven, he never indicated or hinted where heaven was. He certainly talked about heaven on many occasions and urged Christians to look forward to it and to prize heavenly values and standards in their lives here and now. An important aspect of the Lord's teaching on heaven was the comfort and encouragement which were intended for believers. 'Do not let your hearts be troubled,' he directs. 'Trust in God; trust also in me.' He then went on to reassure them about heaven: 'In my Father's house are many rooms; if it were not so, I would have told you. I am going there to prepare a place for you' (John 14:1-2). But the Lord did not elaborate on where heaven was. It was enough to know that heaven existed and that it is a glorious place which the Lord Jesus has prepared for all who love him. What more could one ask for? And, remember, we may be nearer to heaven than we imagine!

9.
God is in heaven as well as everywhere

The preparatory work is complete and we now know the meaning of the various words used in the Bible which are translated as 'heaven'. There is, as we have seen, a range of meanings varying from 'heights', the universe, or the wider expanse of space, to the skies immediately above us and, much more importantly, to a spiritual, non-spatial place where God dwells. It is this latter meaning which the Bible emphasizes and which we too are concentrating on in this book. Not only is heaven where God is, but it is also the place where Christians go to at death.

While God is in heaven, the Bible also teaches that God is everywhere; that is what we mean when we refer to God's omnipresence. But how can God dwell in heaven if, at the same time, he is also present everywhere else? The question is not merely academic because some readers may be genuinely puzzled by what appears, on the surface, to be conflicting strands of teaching in the Bible. There is a further reason why the question is important. If we can understand the significance of these two complementary, not conflicting, teachings then we shall be in a better position to appreciate the fact that heaven is where God dwells.

God is in heaven

We will start from basics. Heaven is God's dwelling-place. 'From heaven', the psalmist informs us, 'the LORD looks down and sees all mankind,' and the point is re-emphasized: 'From his dwelling-place he watches all who live on earth...' (Ps. 33:13,14). The same point is implied in Isaiah's statement: 'For this is what the high and lofty One says — he who lives for ever, whose name is holy: "I live in a high and holy place..." ' (Isa. 57:15). A later reference in prayer by the same prophet is more explicit: 'Look down from heaven and see from your lofty throne, holy and glorious...' (Isa. 63:15).

In a pattern prayer for all his people, the Lord Jesus urges them to begin their prayers with an awareness of their filial relation to God as Father. However, notice where God is: 'Our Father in heaven' (Matt. 6:9).

These references are strengthened by the fact that, as we noted earlier, God is also described in the Bible as the 'God of heaven'. Nehemiah, for example, began praying for his people with the words: 'O Lord, God of heaven...' (Neh. 1:5; see also 2 Chron. 36:23; Ps. 136:26).

Similarly, there is an intimate relationship between the Lord Jesus Christ and heaven. It was from heaven that he came into this world (John 6:33-51; 17:5) and his heavenly origin was evidenced in pronouncements by the Father from heaven (e.g., Matt. 3:16-17; 17:5; John 12:28). Following his resurrection, he ascended into heaven (e.g., Luke 24:51; Acts 1:9; 1 Tim. 3:16; Heb. 9:24) and it is from heaven that Christ will descend again, this time as King and Judge (Acts 1:11; 1 Thess. 4:16; 2 Thess. 1:7).

By now the point has been well established: God is in heaven.

God is everywhere

This point is emphasized in Scripture:

> But will God really dwell on earth? The heavens, even the highest heaven, cannot contain you (1 Kings 8:27).

> Where can I go from your Spirit?
>   Where can I flee from your presence?
> If I go up to the heavens, you are there;
>   if I make my bed in the depths, you are there.
> If I rise on the wings of the dawn,
>   if I settle on the far side of the sea,
> even there your hand will guide me,
>   your right hand will hold me fast
>
>   (Ps. 139:7-10).

> 'Am I only a God nearby,'
>
>   declares the LORD,
>   'and not a God far away?
> Can anyone hide in secret places
>   so that I cannot see him?'
>
>   declares the LORD.
>   'Do not I fill heaven and earth?'
>
>   declares the LORD
>   (Jer. 23:23-24; see also Acts 17:27-28).

Two related terms are used in theology to describe this aspect of God's essential nature: namely, 'immensity', which refers to the perfection of God's being by virtue of which he is outside all limitations of space, time, knowledge and power; and 'omnipresence', which means that God is everywhere, 'present in every point of space with his whole being'.[1] What does this mean?

1. While God is distinct and separate from the world he created, he is still present in every part of it.

2. Size, dimension and distance do not apply to God. He is not confined to any one place, but present in all places at once. Nor does space apply to God; you cannot measure the distance between God and a point in creation, for God is everywhere.

3. God is present everywhere but in different ways in different places. Berkhof is correct in affirming the 'endless variety'[2] of ways in which God is present with his creatures.

4. God is present everywhere in order to retain, rule, reward and reveal.

He is present to retain

This means that the Lord keeps the universe going by upholding and maintaining it: 'All things were created by him and for him. He is before all things, and in him all things hold together' (Col. 1:16-17).

The Lord Jesus, as God, is present to give cohesion, order and sustenance to the whole creation. This is confirmed in Hebrews 1:3: '... sustaining all things by his powerful word'. In other words, he maintains, preserves and directs everything and everyone by his enabling word. The verb 'sustaining' in this text can be translated 'carrying along' and the tense suggests that Christ is continually active in preserving the universe.

He is present to rule

This is what the Puritan Stephen Charnock described as the 'influential omnipresence of God'.[3] He is present with all things by his authority because all are subject to him; his omnipresence is that of a king. 'The Lord reigns' is the repeated message of the Bible (e.g., Ps. 93:1; 97:1; 99:1).

He is present to reward

God is present everywhere and on occasions it is in order to punish people for their disobedience and wickedness. Some famous examples are Adam and Eve (Gen. 3), the Flood (Gen. 6-8), the city of Sodom (Gen. 18-19), Israel in the wilderness (Num. 14:28-30) and the sons of Eli (1 Sam. 2:27-36). Many other Bible examples could be given but the warning is loud and clear. The God who is omnipresent also hates sin and punishes it.

He is present to reveal

In this respect, God's omnipresence varies in different relations as well as in degrees.

     1. God is present in the *church* here to bless and to show more of his mercy, power and glory to his people.
     2. God is present in the *world* to show his goodness, power and eternity.
     3. God is present in *hell* in order to express fully his righteous anger
     4. God is present in *heaven* to show more fully his great love and glory.[4]

God is in heaven as well as everywhere

We have now seen that God is everywhere; he is not confined to heaven. On the other hand, God is in heaven, so what does this mean for our subject? In the words of John Owen, the outstanding Puritan theologian, God is in heaven, not because his being is restricted there, but 'in respect of his eminency or manifestations of himself...'[5] — that is, because he especially and fully shows his glory there to the church. He has appointed heaven as the special place where Christians can see and enjoy their God in the full blaze of his love and glory.

God is not more present in heaven than he is in the world or in hell, yet God is uniquely present in heaven. Why? Because there he displays the glories of his love and mercy to Christians in unlimited and wonderful ways. Think of it in another way. God dwells in his church on earth and this means more than the fact that he is omnipresent. In addition, it means that God is present in his church in a unique way — namely, to show his great covenant love for his people. In heaven, God will show this same covenant love to his people but to a far greater degree and intensity. There will be no need of preachers there, or a Bible, or the symbols of bread and wine. Faith will give way to sight as the believer enters heaven and sees the God of glory in his great love for sinners.

Obviously, God is not only in heaven; he is also in the world and in the church here and now. He is also in hell. But make no mistake about it, God is in heaven in a very special and wonderful way; he is there to show us all his beauty and love. There are unique, continuous, glorious and full manifestations of God and his love in heaven. It will be fantastic!

10.
Heaven and Christ

A well-known Christmas carol begins with the words, 'Once in royal David's city…' Written over a hundred years ago by Cecil Francis Alexander, each of the six verses in this carol is profound and biblical. Notice, for example, how the second verse speaks of Jesus Christ:

> He came down to earth from heaven
> Who is God and Lord of all.

These two lines express briefly but accurately the condescension and deity of Christ. The point is well made too, in many other carols. Consider Charles Wesley's famous carol, 'Hark! the herald angels sing'. The second verse opens like this:

> Christ, by highest heaven adored,
> Christ, the everlasting Lord.

He came from heaven

These writers all agree concerning Jesus Christ: he is God and came from heaven. And that is what the Bible also teaches and implies.

For example, in John 1:18 the Lord Jesus is described as 'God the One and only [Son]'. A more literal translation and reliable textual variant is 'the unique and beloved one [himself] God'.[1] In the same verse Christ is described as being 'at the Father's side' or, even better, 'in the bosom of the Father' (AV). No matter which text is preferred, whether the NIV or the AV, the message of the text is clear: Jesus is in an intimate and eternal relationship with the Father and enjoys 'abiding closeness'[2] with him. Jesus Christ, then, is one who is 'most intimately united from all eternity to God the Father, and is equal to him in all things'.[3]

Or think of another example from the same Gospel where the Lord Jesus prays these words: 'And now, Father, glorify me in your presence with the glory I had with you before the world began' (John 17:5). Unlike humans, Christ existed in heaven eternally, long 'before the world began' and before he was born of the virgin Mary. Ryle's comment at this point is fair: 'Sayings like these can only be used of one who is very God. To no patriarch, or prophet, or king, or apostle, is any such language ever applied in the Bible. It belongs to none but God.'[4] In other words, not only was Jesus Christ pre-existent in heaven, but he was also equal to the Father in a gloriously intimate and perfect relationship.

Yes, heaven was and remains Christ's home. He had always been there. And it was from heaven he came at the time of his first advent. As many as six times in John 6:33-51 the Lord Jesus refers to himself as 'the bread of God ... who *comes down from heaven...*' (italics mine). Or again, in a later chapter, Jesus distinguishes himself from his Jewish critics. 'You are from below,' he pointedly remarked. 'I am from above. You are of this world; I am not of this world' (John 8:23). A little later he told the same people, 'I came from God and now am here' (8:42; cf. 13:3).

The message could not be clearer: Christ did not begin to exist in the womb of Mary or at Bethlehem. Nor was this world his real home. As God the Son he had come down from heaven where he had always been with his Father.

He received approval from heaven

On several occasions, heaven bore remarkable witness to Jesus Christ during his earthly ministry. One occasion was at the commencement of his ministry when he was baptized. At a personal level there was no need at all for him to be baptized. After all, he had no need to repent or receive forgiveness, for he was perfect. But to the surprise of John the Baptist, Jesus insisted on being baptized. Why did he do this? He was identifying himself with sinners and as their representative and substitute he would die on the cross bearing their guilt and punishment. As he began publicly this task of preaching and later dying, 'The heaven was opened' and the voice of God the Father, 'from heaven, said, "This is my Son, whom I love; with him I am well pleased" ' (Matt. 3:17) — a special moment indeed for a very special person undertaking a special, unique mission.

Another occasion was shortly after the halfway stage in his ministry had been reached. In order to get away from the crowds for the purpose of praying, the Lord Jesus walked with three of his disciples up a mountain called Hermon, which was about 9,000 feet above sea level. As Jesus prayed on the mountain, 'The appearance of his face changed, and his clothes became as bright as a flash of lightning' (Luke 9:28-29). It was not a freak, nor did Jesus change into a ghost. What happened was a brief but partial unveiling of Christ's glory as God. The disciples saw it and Peter reported, 'We were eyewitnesses of his majesty.' They also heard the 'voice that came from heaven' which declared, 'This is my Son, whom I love; with him I am well pleased' (2 Peter 1:16-18). The one from heaven received the approval of heaven once again.

A third occasion occurred only a couple of days before Jesus died on the cross. After talking about his approaching death, Jesus gave expression to his own inner turmoil and horrors concerning the impending cross. In reaffirming his purpose to die, he prayed, 'Father, glorify your name!' It was at this point that 'A voice came from heaven' (John 12:28) affirming, 'I have glorified it, and will glorify it again.' This message from heaven was clear. God the Father's name had already been honoured and displayed through the life, teaching and miracles of the Lord Jesus. That was a fact. But now the promise was that the Father would be honoured further in the sufferings and death of his Son as well as in his resurrection and ascension.

These three special occasions indicate the equality of the Father and Son as well as their intimate, permanent relationship. In addition, they point to the Son's heavenly origin and express the Father's complete approval of the Son as the Saviour of sinners as he faced and consented to death.

His return to heaven

It is the ascension, however, which even more strongly identifies heaven with the Lord Jesus; it also proves he had come from heaven. Jesus made this very point, for example, in John 6:62, when he said, 'What if you see the Son of Man ascend to where he was before!' 'Other religious leaders,' writes D. A. Carson, 'were said to have ascended to heaven at the end of their life, but Jesus the Son of Man ... first *descended* (v. 38), and so in ascending is merely returning to *where he was before*. This not only affirms Jesus' pre-existence, but places him in a class quite different from antecedent Jewish religious heroes.'[5]

Repeatedly Jesus spoke of returning to the Father in heaven. 'I am with you for only a short time,' he said, 'and then I go to the one who sent me' (John 7:33; see also 14:12,28). Three times in a later chapter Jesus speaks of returning to the Father: 'Now I am going to him who sent me... I am going to the Father... I am leaving the world and going back to the Father' (John 16:5,10,28: see also 16:17; 20:17). The emphasis here is significant.

The narrative accounts relating the return of the Lord Jesus to heaven are recorded in Luke 24:50-53 and Acts 1:9-11. While the first narrative closes Christ's ministry on earth, the account in Acts, which is more detailed, introduces the ascension of Jesus as leading to his ministry in heaven as mediator on behalf of the church in the world. There are five significant statements for us to notice in these two narratives.

First of all, we are told that 'he left' the disciples (Luke 24:51), and in Acts 1 the details are provided for us. The disciples were astonished as they watched him leaving them. They would not see him again until they themselves died and went to heaven.

Secondly, we are told that 'he was taken up' (Luke 24:51; Acts 1:2,9). The verb here is in the passive voice indicating that the ascension of Jesus, like his resurrection, was an act of God the Father. Jesus was ready to go back to heaven on Easter Sunday but he stayed for nearly six weeks in order to give the disciples proof of his resurrection and to teach, encourage and prepare them for their future work.

Thirdly, both narratives emphasize the fact that Jesus went 'into heaven'. He went home as Victor and Lord to receive the acclaim and welcome of heaven.

Fourthly, we are informed that 'A cloud hid him from their sight.' In addition to curbing the curiosity of the disciples, the cloud symbolized the divine presence and glory. It was an awesome and deeply significant moment.

Finally, as the disciples stood astonished looking at the ascent of Jesus to heaven, two angels 'stood beside them' and announced, 'This same Jesus, who has been taken from you into heaven, will come back in the same way you have seen him go into heaven' (Acts 1:11). Notice the words, 'will come back in the same way'. Those words are pregnant with meaning as his ascension and second coming are compared. He will return 'in the same way', but there will also be differences. Jesus ascended privately and on his own, with only a small number of disciples witnessing the event. However, when he returns from heaven as King to usher in the end of the world he will not be on his own; the angels, archangels and even Christians already in heaven will return with him (Matt. 25:31; 1 Thess. 4:13-18). And there will be many witnesses. In fact, the Bible declares that 'Every eye will see him' (Rev. 1:7). But that is not all. Everyone in the world will bow and confess Jesus as Lord (Phil. 2:10-11). The Lord of heaven will then be duly acknowledged by all.

His heavenly ministry

Until that glorious day when he steps out of heaven in glory, the Lord Jesus continues in heaven. His presence and ministry there are crucial for us. He rules, quickens, gifts, protects and prays for his people, governing all things for their good (Matt. 28:18; Eph. 1:20-23; 4:11-12). All that we need to reach heaven is supplied by our Lord who is in heaven.

11.
Heaven: where it will be

Heaven is essentially where God is; it is also a place but is spiritual and not spatial or temporal. These are the main points which have been underlined in the last two chapters. Before considering the implications of the fact that God is in heaven, we need to discuss a further question in relation to where heaven will be in the future. Perhaps you do not understand the question and I need to express it differently. Well, the Bible states that when the Lord Jesus returns personally at the end of history there will then be 'a new heaven and a new earth, the home of righteousness' (2 Peter 3:13). What does this mean with regard to heaven in the future? Will heaven be different? And what does it say, if anything, about heaven's future location? Here Christians disagree in their answers and we need to proceed with caution and charity in discussing these questions.

James Packer confidently claims that heaven 'will take the form of a reconstructed cosmos'.[1] A. A. Hodge is less dogmatic but affirms that 'a strong probability is raised' that the location of the place where Christ and his church have their 'central home throughout eternity ... will be our present earth, first burned with fire and then gloriously replenished'.[2] William Hendriksen agrees: The 'gloriously renewed universe will be ours to enjoy and to use for the glory of God ... we shall be adapted to this new universe.'[3] A similar approach is taken by Herman Hoeksema. From 2 Peter 3:13 and Revelation 6:14, Hoeksema concludes that 'The Lord shall cause a new cosmos to appear, the new heavens and the new earth.'[4] However, he issues a helpful warning: 'We must beware that we do not form an earthly conception of this new and heavenly kingdom.' Without speculating concerning the nature of the new heaven and new earth, Hoeksema believes that 'In the most literal sense of the word heavenly conditions and heavenly relationships shall exist on the new earth, and there will be an immediate relation between the new earth and the new heaven above.'[5]

Wayne Grudem concurs with this position. He insists that 'Heaven is even now a place — though one whose location is now unknown to us and whose existence is now unable to be perceived by our natural senses.' This is correct and the point was emphasized earlier. Grudem, however, goes on to explain: 'It is this place of God's dwelling that will be somehow made new at the time of the final judgement and will be joined to a renewed earth.'[6] Grudem believes that there will be 'a place and activities'[7] for our new resurrection bodies as Christians in the new heavens and new earth, including eating and drinking, 'musical and artistic activities',[8] as well as the 'whole range of investigation and development of the creation by technological, creative and inventive means'.

Not all the writers quoted above agree with Grudem in his detailed expectations of the activities and life of believers on the new earth. They all agree, however, that the heavens in some way will be reconstructed and either joined to a new earth or an 'immediate relation' will be established between the new earth and the new heaven. And on the new earth only heavenly conditions will exist. This is an intriguing subject and in the next chapter we will examine in more detail the biblical basis for this expectation. For the rest of this chapter it will be helpful to pause and remind ourselves of the biblical context in which the 'new heaven and new earth' will occur. In other words we will mention some basic Bible facts concerning the end of the world.

One thing is clear: this world will not carry on for ever, at least not in its present form. And that is not my view; it is what the Bible teaches. Let me explain this simply. God is continually working his purposes out in our world. Nothing happens by chance or by fate. All events, people and nations are under the absolute control of God; the strangest and most unexpected circumstances, or even wicked people, are also used by God to achieve his plans. God 'works out everything in conformity with the purpose of his will' (Eph. 1:11). Quite often we do not understand what God is doing in our lives or in the world generally, for his ways are past finding out (Rom. 11:33; Isa. 55:8-9). He is infinitely wise and plans all things perfectly. Nor will God fail to carry out his plans. 'My purpose will stand,' says the Lord, 'and I will do all that I please' (Isa. 46:10) even through, and despite, human sin and rebellion.

An important part of God's plan is that a vast number of people whom he has chosen should be saved and eventually go to heaven. As the *Westminster Confession of Faith* declares, 'It pleased God, in his eternal purpose, to choose and ordain the Lord Jesus, his only begotten Son, to be the mediator between God and man.'[9] That work Christ accomplished by his death as their substitute on the cross. He thereby 'purchased not only reconciliation,' the confession rightly insists, 'but an everlasting inheritance in the kingdom of heaven, for all those whom the Father has given unto him.'[10] Not only are such people reborn by the Holy Spirit, justified freely by grace, forgiven of all their sins, adopted into God's family as children, sanctified and also kept by God's power, but they are also taken safely into heaven when they die.

Nor is that the end. There is even more to come. And the scope of all that God will do for Christians is summarized briefly in Romans 8:30: 'And those he predestined, he also called; those he called, he also justified; those he justified, he also glorified.' Notice that last word, 'glorified'; it is important but frequently overlooked. This word refers to the very last part of our total redemption. Let me explain. Although Christians go immediately to heaven when they die and are perfect in holiness, enjoying the sight and fellowship of Christ, yet there is even more to come. It is staggering and almost unbelievable, but it is true. What else then will God do for Christians? Put it like this: Christ has redeemed us from sin, but he has also redeemed us from the consequences of sin, including physical death. 'The last enemy to be destroyed,' announces the apostle Paul, 'is death' (1 Cor. 15:26). When will this happen? The Bible's answer is clear and emphatic. Referring to the personal return of the Lord Jesus to this world, the apostle Paul writes, 'And we eagerly await a Saviour from there [heaven], the Lord Jesus Christ, who, by the power that enables him to bring everything under his control, will transform our lowly bodies so that they will be like his glorious body' (Phil. 3:20-21). Consider a more detailed and exciting statement:

> I declare to you, brothers, that flesh and blood cannot inherit the kingdom of God, nor does the perishable inherit the imperishable. Listen, I tell you a mystery: We will not all sleep, but we will all be changed — in a flash, in the twinkling of an eye, at the last trumpet. For the trumpet will sound, the dead will be raised imperishable, and we will be changed... When the perishable has been clothed with the imperishable, and the mortal with immortality, then the saying that is written will come true: 'Death has been swallowed up in victory.'

'Where, O death, is your victory?
Where, O death, is your sting?'

The sting of death is sin, and the power of sin is the law.
But thanks be to God! He gives us the victory through
our Lord Jesus Christ (1 Cor. 15:50-57).

To be glorified, then, means that our bodies will also be
raised and made like the glorious body of Christ. Yes, 'The
dead in Christ will rise' (1 Thess. 4:16). And it will happen to
all Christians *together* and at the same time. Although we may
have been converted to Christ at different times and also die
and go to heaven on our own at varying times, yet we shall be
raised and glorified together.

But there is even more! When Christians are glorified, creation itself will also be renewed: 'The creation itself will be
liberated from its bondage to decay and brought into the glorious freedom of the children of God' (Rom. 8:21). When will
this happen? Just two verses later we are told that creation
will be transformed at the time of 'the redemption of our bodies'. That is why the Bible speaks of 'new heavens and a new
earth' (2 Peter 3:13) which will be the result of this cosmic
renewal and regeneration. All this will take place in the future,
but only when the Lord Jesus returns visibly and in glory. To
this great climactic event, Christians can eagerly look forward.

Having now provided the wider biblical context, in the next
chapter we will continue to probe the significance of this future hope of 'new heavens and a new earth' for the location of
heaven. Our question then remains, *where* will heaven be?

12.
Heaven: an intermediate state

We are still discussing the intriguing question as to where heaven will be in the future, after the Lord's return, especially in the light of the statement that there will then be 'a new heaven and a new earth, the home of righteousness' (2 Peter 3:13). What does this mean with regard to heaven in the future? That is the question we shall discuss in this chapter and the next one. All we attempted to do in the previous chapter was to introduce the question before placing this eschatological event in the context of the Lord's second and personal coming to this world in glory. Christians disagree in their interpretation of 2 Peter 3:13 and the relationship of heaven to this new earth but we will now attempt to understand the claim that heaven is an intermediate state between death and the resurrection. For convenience this will be referred to as position 'A'.

Summary of this position

The view of heaven as an intermediate state can be summarized briefly as follows, with reference to a number of modern writers:

1. Until the Second Coming of Christ, Christians go to heaven when they die. This is the 'intermediate state between death and resurrection', but their happiness in heaven 'will be provisional and incomplete'.[1]

2. For 'the completion of their happiness', Christians 'await the resurrection of the body and the new earth which God will create as the culmination of his redemptive work'.[2]

3. 'Christians often talk about living with God "in heaven" for ever. But in fact the biblical teaching is richer than that: it tells us that there will be new heavens *and a new earth* — an entirely new creation — and we will live with God there.'[3]

4. Many 'believe that when the Christian dies he goes to be with Christ; and they seem to think of that as some vague, nebulous, indefinite spiritual state and condition. But that is not the teaching of the Scripture. The Scripture teaches the resurrection of the body as an essential part of our salvation ... we shall dwell in these glorified bodies on the glorified earth. This is one of the great Christian doctrines that has been almost entirely forgotten and ignored.'[4]

5. 'As I understand it, what is commonly described as "heaven" in the Scripture is what we should regard as the intermediate state, not the final state, not the eternal state. I mean that what is generally described as "heaven" in the Scripture is the condition described by Paul in Philippians 1:23, where he talks about being "with Christ, which is far better". That is the intermediate state for this good reason, that in the eternal and final state, the body is involved. But when he talks about "being with Christ, which is far better", the body is not involved. The body may be in a grave, it may be in the depths of the sea somewhere, it may have been blown to atoms.

He is not referring there to the body. That is the intermediate state, the state and condition of the redeemed
while they are waiting for the resurrection of the body
and its final glorification.'[5]

6. 'Heaven is not the ultimate goal or resting place
for the Christian.'[6]

My purpose in using these quotations has been to allow the
advocates of position 'A' to express their views succinctly and
briefly. I am not suggesting that these are the only advocates
of the view that heaven is an intermediate state, but they are
representative of theologians who have wrestled with the subject and arrived at a clearly articulated version of what I call
position 'A'.

Arguments in favour of this view

I now intend to identify and outline their most important arguments for position 'A'.

1. The creation mandate

From Genesis 1:28 we 'learn that God promised man nothing
less than the earth itself as his proper habitation and inheritance'.[7] Man's creation mandate from God his Creator was to
rule over all the earth.

2. God's curse on creation since man's original fall into sin
(Gen. 3:17-19)

'The fact that earth had been cursed on account of man's sin
would also seem to imply that, as a part of the promised victory, this curse and all the other results of sin which the curse

involved would be removed. In a sense, therefore, the expectation of a new earth was already implicit in the promise of Genesis 3:15.'[8]

'When humanity fell ... we brought down the whole of creation with us; the curse fell on the very dust from which we emerged as well as on ourselves. Subjection, bondage and decay were all elements in Adam's experience and the fruit of his sin. This fall was reversed by Jesus Christ... The full effects of Christ's reversal of the fall will finally emerge in the resurrection change. The whole cosmos will share in this resurrection change and will itself be renewed.'[9]

'This extraordinary doctrine of the intimate connection between man and creation ... when he fell all that was under him fell with him, and became a creation which is "subject to vanity" and which is "in the bondage of corruption". We see then the unity between man and his surroundings, the creation. What happens to man happens to it both negatively and positively. That is why the whole creation is "earnestly expecting", craning its neck, waiting with eager expectation for the manifestation of the sons of God.'[10]

3. Old Testament teaching concerning the inheritance of the land

In the Old Testament era, the inheritance of the land (Gen. 17:8) was limited to Canaan, 'whereas in New Testament times the inheritance is expanded to include the entire earth'.[11] Abraham's expectation of the promise's fulfilment is explained in Hebrews 11:9-10, especially the words: 'He was looking forward to the city with foundations, whose architect and builder is God,' that is, 'the new Jerusalem which will be found on the earth'.[12] Also, Hebrews 4 pictures the earthly Canaan as 'a type of the eternal Sabbath rest'. For this reason, Canaan 'was not an end in itself; it pointed forward to the new earth

which was to come'.[13] Galatians 3:29 teaches that Christians
are Abraham's seed and 'The promise of which we are heirs
must include the promise of the land,' that is, the new earth.

4. Prophecies of the new earth in Isaiah

Important prophetic passages in Isaiah 11:6-9; 35:1-2; 55:12-
13; 65:17-25; 66:22-23 speak of the new earth.

Oliphint and Ferguson rightly see these statements, especially 65:17-25, as being 'behind'[14] New Testament references like 2 Peter 3:10-13, but are unsure 'whatever measure
of fulfilment this [Isa. 65:17-25] may already have in the
church...'[15]

Hoekema argues that what is predicted in Isaiah 66:22-23
'is the perpetual worship of all the people of God, gathered
from all nations, in ways which will be suitable to the glorious
new existence they will enjoy on the new earth'.[16]

These prophecies from Isaiah refer to a new earth which
will last for ever and not to a thousand-year millennium.[17] Arguments in support of this are as follows:

a. The millennium is regarded as 'a temporary condition' of one thousand years followed by conflict and
sin, but 'there is nothing of a temporary nature about
the glory' described in Romans 8:18-23 or Isaiah 65.

b. The only reference in the Bible to a thousand-year
period is Revelation 20:2-6 but 'There is no reference
whatsoever to the condition of creation.' Numbers in
Revelation are symbolic and the figure ten expresses
symbolically the idea of completeness. When ten is multiplied by ten and again by ten it represents a very long
period.

c. There is no reference to a thousand-year period on
earth in Isaiah 11 or anywhere else in the Bible.

6. New Testament passages

Matthew 19:28: 'At the renewal of all things, when the Son of Man sits on his glorious throne...' In this 'renewal' or 'regeneration' all things are made new[18] but only when the Lord Jesus returns in glory.

Acts 3:21: 'He must remain in heaven until the time comes for God to restore everything, as he promised long ago through his holy prophets.' Simon J. Kistemaker comments that 'The times of refreshing that come as a result of repentance and faith are harbingers of the time of complete restoration. Whereas the seasons of refreshing are periodic and subjective, the time of restoration is permanent and objective.'[19] Hoekema believes that this restoration points 'to the new earth'.[20]

Romans 8:18-23, where 'Paul describes the expectation of the new earth by the present creation in vivid terms.'[21]

2 Peter 3:10-13 is a more detailed description. 'Peter's point', writes A. A. Hoekema, 'is that, though the present earth will be "burned up", God will give us new heavens and a new earth which will never be destroyed but will last for ever.'[22] Bernard Ramm reminds us that 'The promise mentioned by Peter can only mean the promises of the Old Testament, for he also uses the rich Old Testament expression, "the day of the Lord".'[23]

Revelation 4; 5; 6, especially 6:9-11. The scene in chapter 6 is very different from that in chapter 5; in the latter, believers were occupied exclusively with praise to God but in chapter 6 they are crying out to the Lord (v. 10). 'This vision shows us that heaven is not the ultimate goal or resting place for the Christian. Even those in heaven continue to pray that God's kingdom will come.'[24]

Revelation 21; 22. Here we have a picture of 'the new heavens and earth as a magnificent cosmos in which all that was ruined in the old is repaired and beautified...'[25] In 21:9, 'We find an extraordinary description of the inheritance ... in symbolic form, of course.'[26] Hoekema thinks that 21:1-4 contains 'the most breathtaking description of the new earth in the entire Bible'.[27] The following points are underlined by various writers:

1. The 'new Jerusalem' (21:2-7) refers to the time when we shall have a new resurrection body, on a new earth, under new heavens, wherein dwells righteousness.[28]

2. The dwelling-place of God 'will no longer be away from the earth but on the earth. Since where God dwells, there heaven is, we conclude that in the life to come heaven and earth will no longer be separated, as they are now, but *will be merged*. Believers will therefore continue to be in heaven as they continue to live on the new earth' (see Rev. 21:3 — italics mine).[29]

Grudem, in this context, talks of 'a new kind of unification of heaven and earth ... a joining of heaven and earth in this new creation, and there we will live in the presence of God'.[30]

3. What is of greatest importance is Revelation 21:3: 'Now the dwelling of God is with men, and he will live with them...'[31]

Having now identified the main arguments for position 'A', namely, heaven as an *intermediate* state, we will turn in the next chapter to arguments in favour of heaven as an *eternal* state.

13.
Heaven: an eternal state

In this chapter we are discussing a slightly different view, which I am calling position 'B', in which heaven is regarded as an eternal, not an intermediate, state.

However, some preliminary remarks are necessary before we proceed further. Firstly, there is a clear and urgent challenge for us to search and interpret the Bible thoroughly in order to ascertain what it actually teaches. Are we guilty of reading the Bible superficially and selectively? Have we grappled, for example, with the concept of the new heaven and new earth? I still remember quite vividly an occasion some years ago when a Jehovah Witness leader challenged me to explain the meaning of the Lord's words: 'Blessed are the meek, for *they will inherit the earth*' (Matt. 5:5, italics mine). The opening words were familiar to me but I had completely ignored the rest of the verse. I had been caught out! But, secondly, the subject we are considering is important in order to understand and appreciate the scope, as well as the magnitude, of God's redemptive purpose in Christ. This purpose is far from being merely individualistic and subjective; it is corporate, cosmic, cataclysmic and renovative. It really is exciting, but have I taken the trouble to try to understand this glorious purpose of God? Here is a challenge for us all to study the Bible more carefully and thoroughly.

Summary of position 'B'

The view of heaven as an eternal state is summarized briefly here by referring to the writings of Jonathan Edwards, the eighteenth-century American theologian and pastor:

1. 'The place of the abode of the saints after the resurrection will be in heaven, as well as before.'[1]
2. 'The world of the blessed, that is, the new world, or the new heavens and earth ... is heaven.'
3. 'Is it likely that God should change the place of his eternal abode and remove, and come and dwell in another part of the universe?'[2]
4. 'The place of God's eternal residence, and the place of the everlasting residence and reign of Christ, and his church, will be heaven, and not this world, purified and refined.'[3]

Arguments in favour of this view

1. The believer possesses all things in Christ

'By virtue of the believer's union with Christ, he really possesses all things.'[4] How? 'God, three in one, all that he is, and all that he has, and all that he does, all that he has made ... are as much the Christian's... All the universe is his... Christ ... manages it for him... This is the kingdom Christ so often promised ... this is the sitting in Christ's throne, and inheriting all things promised to the victors in the Revelation...'

A variation of this view was taught by Martyn Lloyd-Jones in the early period of his ministry in expounding Matthew 5:5: 'Blessed are the meek, for they will inherit the earth.'[5] He argues:

'The meek already inherit the earth in this life' because they are always satisfied and contented.

The apostle Paul illustrates this in Philippians 4: 'I know what it is to be in need, and I know what it is to have plenty' (v. 12). '... I am amply supplied...' (v. 18).

The apostle Paul underlines the point in 1 Corinthians 3:21-22: 'All things are yours ... all are yours, and you are of Christ, and Christ is of God.'

Charles Hodge explains the significance of these words.[6] 'All things' includes the ministry which belongs to the church; the world in its widest sense, directed to promote the great work of salvation and the church; life and death are purposeful and also dispensed so as best to fulfil the designs of the church; things present and future are all permanently subject to the church, while the church is subject to, and belongs to, Christ, and to no one else.

Lloyd-Jones acknowledges that Matthew 5:5 'has a future reference also' although, apart from quoting 1 Corinthians 6:2-3 and saying that Christians inherit the earth by judging angels in the future, he does not give any detailed treatment of the words. His revised and detailed position is provided in his commentary on Romans 8:18-23.

2. The promise of an eternal house

As believers, 'We have a building from God, an eternal house in heaven...' (2 Cor. 5:1). 'If,' writes Edwards, 'the saints' abode in heaven be temporary as well as their abode on earth ... their house there would be but a *tabernacle* as well as here. By the *house eternal in the heavens*, it is evident there is some respect had to the resurrection body, which proves that the place of the abode of the saints after the resurrection will be in heaven, as well as before.'[7]

3. The promise of a future inheritance

'If Christians were only to stay in heaven until the resurrection, then they would be pilgrims and strangers in heaven, as well as on earth, and the country that the saints of old declared plainly that they sought ... will be but a temporary Canaan, as well as the earth.'[8]

'The Lord from heaven does not come to give his elect the country of the earthly Adam only renewed...' See Colossians 1:5: 'the hope that is stored up for you in heaven...' also Matthew 5:12: '... because great is your reward in heaven'. Our inheritance is also being 'kept in heaven' (1 Peter 1:4) and Christians are directed to 'Store up for yourselves treasures in heaven' (Matt. 6:20).

4. Christ entered heaven as our forerunner

'Christ ascended into heaven as the forerunner of the church; and therefore the whole church shall enter there... Christ entered into heaven with his risen and glorified body, as an earnest of the same resurrection and ascension to the bodies of the saints; therefore, when the bodies of the saints shall rise, they shall also ascend into heaven.'

5. There is progress as well as new joys in heaven

'The addition of happiness and glory made to the saints at the resurrection,' writes Edwards, 'will be exceeding great'[9] and will consist partly in the following factors: glorified bodies of believers, the church being complete and perfect, the Mediator having fully accomplished his work and triumphing over all his enemies, the consummation of God's purposes. And then, 'God will make more abundant manifestations of his glory, and of the glory of his Son ... a joyful occasion as the finishing

of all things and the marriage of the Lamb... This will be the
wedding-day between Christ and the Church, and this wedding-day will last for ever...'

6. How are the Old Testament prophecies to be understood?

The Old Testament background to 2 Peter 3:13 needs to be
interpreted responsibly and carefully.

Competent commentators and theologians are extremely
cautious in interpreting the Isaiah passages which are 'behind'
2 Peter 3:13. For example, A. A. Hoekema acknowledges:
'Whether they are all to be *literally* fulfilled is open to question; surely details about wolves and lambs, and about mountains dropping sweet wine, are to be understood not in a crassly
literal way but as figurative descriptions of what the new earth
will be like.'[10] Charles Hodge is also somewhat uncertain as to
whether these prophecies are 'intended merely as an exornation
[that is, adornment]... or whether ... didactic...'[11] (italics mine).

In addition to the caution of the above writers, there is also
a strong note of uncertainty as to the degree in which these
prophecies have already been fulfilled in the 'here and now' in
the gospel age. While Hendriksen thinks Isaiah 11:6-8 will
reach its *'ultimate* fulfilment' in the new earth, he nevertheless concedes that 'There is an anticipatory fulfilment in the
present dispensation, ushered in by the coming of Christ into
the flesh.'[12] He also acknowledges that even with regard to
the 'ultimate fulfilment' Isaiah 11:6-8 'is set forth in *symbolic
language*'. I agree; the wolf and the lamb, the calf and the lion
represent a spiritual reality. These images must not be pressed
literally for they are intended to represent the total transformation of reality and the end of hostilities. Oliphint and
Ferguson are not clear what 'measure of fulfilment' Isaiah
65:17-25 'may already have in the church'.[13]

Certainly a number of contrasts are intended in these Old Testament prophecies. In Psalm 102:26, for example, there is a contrast between the present temporary creation and the unchanging God and his covenant love, whereas Isaiah 65:17-25 contrasts the troubles of the church in the world and the glorious change the Lord will achieve. Isaiah 66:22 is an even more difficult statement to interpret. The context is one of judgement and hope; verse 19 is representative of the Gentiles and then the sufferings of Israel are contrasted with the ultimate victory and unchanging blessings of God upon his people. Interestingly, the two statements in Isaiah relating to 'the new heavens and the new earth' (65:17; 66:22) are extremely brief and also vague, so that considerable care is needed in interpreting these prophecies.

Conclusion: weighing up the two views

Areas of agreement

In contrasting positions 'A' and 'B', it should be apparent by now that there is considerable agreement between the advocates of both positions.

1. Both agree that glory awaits all Christians, and only Christians, immediately at death and also at the *parousia* (that is, appearing) of the Lord Jesus.
2. There is also a common emphasis on glorification and the ultimate victory of Christ over all his enemies, including death.
3. The curse pronounced by God on creation at the time of man's first sin will also be reversed at the appearing of Christ in glory when there will be a new heaven

and a new earth; both positions 'A' and 'B' agree fully
with this.

4. Agreement is often shared too, concerning degrees
of glory in heaven prior to, and after, the resurrection of
the body and the cosmic regeneration.

Disagreement

The main disagreement focuses on whether heaven for Chris-
tians is only an intermediate state existing until the return of
Christ or whether it is eternal and, even with glorified bodies,
Christians will remain in heaven rather than on the new earth.

The strengths of position 'A'

One immediate strength of this position is the way in which it
seeks to do justice to an important strand of biblical teaching,
especially in the Old Testament, relating to the land which was
integral in the covenant with Abraham. As we have seen, a
strong case is made via Galatians 3, Hebrews 4 and 11 that
this promise relates to the new earth.

An appropriate stress is placed on future cosmic regeneration from statements in Matthew 19, Acts 3, Romans 8 and
2 Peter 3. One wonders whether position 'B' does justice to
these verses and includes a sufficiently biblical resurrection
perspective on the eternal state or not.

The arguments from Revelation 6:9-11 and chapters 21 and
22 are challenging and almost persuasive; advocates of position 'B' need to give more attention to the argument especially
from Revelation 6:9-11.

The strengths of position 'B'

One major strength is the emphasis on continuity in heaven in
the periods prior to, and following, Christ's second advent.

Have advocates of position 'A' shown conclusively that heaven is *only* an intermediate state?

The relationship between heaven and the new earth is, Lloyd-Jones admits, 'a difficult subject'[14] and, later, he confesses, 'We do not know, and I cannot give details about the relationship between that glorified earth and the heavens.'[15] The honesty here is admirable and necessary but advocates of position 'A', including Lloyd-Jones, have their suggestions to make. By contrast, advocates of position 'B' seem less concerned to describe this relationship and do not give way to conjecture.

Is the logic of position 'A' always biblical? For example, one writer argues that 'There must be a glorified earth in which we are to live in our glorified bodies.'[16] I am not convinced by the logic, for there may be an underlying confusion in applying spatial categories to what is really non-spatial or spiritual.

In conclusion, rather than taking sides at this stage, I urge you to search the Scriptures and weigh carefully these different arguments. Whichever of these two positions you may adopt, remember that heaven is going to be fantastic!

14.
Heaven: when Christians go there

John Bradford was aged about thirty-five. A well-educated man and a chaplain to Bishop Ridley, Bradford was a committed Protestant Christian. His conversion had been remarkable and his life transformed by Christ. He soon earned a reputation for being a great preacher and his delight was to proclaim the gospel of God's free grace in Christ. However, only four weeks after Queen Mary commenced her reign in England, this young preacher was imprisoned by the Roman Catholic authorities. Early in July 1555, he was burnt at the stake in Smithfield, London, as a Protestant martyr. He felt honoured to be able to die for Christ. As the flames of the fire began to scorch his body, Bradford spoke his last words to the other young man dying with him: 'Be of good comfort, brother; for we shall have a merry supper with the Lord this night.'[1] He was in no doubt where he was going. And he knew when he was going to heaven — immediately or, in his own words, 'this night'.

Or think of Billy Bray, the rugged Cornish tin-miner converted to Christ early in the nineteenth century. As he approached his seventy-fourth birthday in 1868, Billy began to feel very ill and told some friends, 'I think I shall be home to Father's house soon.' A doctor examined him and announced to Billy, 'You are going to die.' The patient immediately shouted out with joy, 'Glory! Glory be to God! I shall soon be in heaven.' For Bray, there was no doubt about it. As a Christian, he knew that dying meant going to heaven — and 'soon', not just in the distant future.

We need to probe further at this point. Were John Bradford and Billy Bray correct in thinking that they would go straight to heaven when they died? And how can we know whether they were correct or not? Are there not other views?

Purgatory

There certainly are other views. One such view is that many people when they die go to a place called purgatory. As formulated by the Roman Catholic Church, purgatory is an abode available after death to the imperfect 'faithful' of the Roman church; it is preparatory to heaven, and here people stay for longer or shorter periods until their sins are purged. The implications of this teaching encourage, for example, prayers for the dead and indulgences, as well as contributing to a lack of assurance and radically undermining the Saviour's sacrifice on the cross in terms of its finality and sufficiency.

Roman Catholics appeal to tradition and Scripture in order to support and explain their teaching on purgatory. Their appeal to Matthew 3:11 (especially the words, 'He will baptize you with the Holy Spirit and with fire') is irresponsible, while 1 Corinthians 3:11-15 refers to ministers of the gospel and their responsibility to do their work well in view of the fact that they will be judged by the Lord Jesus. There is no reference at all here to purgatory. Nor do the statements in 1 Peter 3:18-20 support the notion of purgatory. Peter's purpose here is to encourage his readers in their persecution and he reminds them of the approaching judgement. The message of these verses is that Christ has suffered and died in the flesh for our sin (v. 18). What he did in his earthly ministry, such as preaching, he now continues to do, but in the Holy Spirit and through the apostles. A parallel situation was the judgement and the flood in the days of Noah; but before that judgement too, Christ preached in the spirit through Noah, and he and his family were saved. Similarly, through baptism into Christ's body these early Christians were secure eternally, even in the face of physical death. Later, in 1 Peter 4:6, Peter refers to Christians who, though physically dead, were alive to God in glory, so that physical death had not deprived them of salvation. The gospel had been preached to them before their death, so that the judgement due to them as sinners was accomplished while they were in this world, that is, 'in the flesh'.

Clearly then, purgatory finds no support at all in the Bible. Professor Paul Helm rightly concludes that 'Scripture nowhere teaches there is to be a period of moral purifying for anyone after death.'[2]

Reincarnation

But what about reincarnation? This theory has been popularized over the past twenty-five years in the West by a growing number of movements originating in the East, or movements which have been influenced by Eastern religions. Yoga, for example, teaches that there will be eventual reincarnations for human beings in new human or animal bodies for as long as is necessary. Hare Krishna devotees believe that future reincarnations on earth await all those who allow passion to rule their lives here. Theosophy, a cult closely akin to spiritism, teaches that people achieve their own salvation through numerous re-incarnations. The New Age Movement, which emerged in the 1970s, expects repeated reincarnations which form a spiritual path, or *sadhana*. Normally spiritual development is believed to occur after several lifetimes in a physical body.

Once again the important issue is not whether a guru or cult propounds the theory, or whether it appeals to some people, but rather whether the Bible teaches reincarnation. We must be guided by God in his Word, not by the fallible, changing opinions of men. And the Bible leaves us in no doubt on the subject. Reincarnation is wrong. Death and the grave are described in the Bible as 'the place of no return' (Job 10:21); 'He who goes down to the grave does not return' (Job 7:9-10), no, not in any form. In fact, 'Man is destined to die *once*, and after that to face judgement' (Heb. 9:27).

One reason given in support of reincarnation is the injustice and unfairness which characterize human life on earth. This theory wrongly claims that these injustices are rectified by the purging and rewards of different reincarnations for the people concerned. Again the Bible rejects this theory. Jesus Christ is the Judge and he will reward all people according to their works (see John 5:22,27; Rom. 2:2-10; 1 Peter 1:17; Matt. 25:31-33). All the injustices, corruption and unfairness which characterize human life and society will be judged when individuals die and then, finally, when the Lord Jesus returns gloriously to earth one day. There is no need of reincarnation to effect justice and fair play in the world, for 'God ... has set a day when he will judge the world with justice by the man he has appointed' (Acts 17:30-31). On that future day, Christ will make a new heaven and a new earth, the home of righteousness (2 Peter 3:13).

To those who believe in Jesus Christ an abundant entrance is given, not into purgatory or a reincarnated life, but into heaven itself (2 Peter 1:11). On the other hand, hell awaits unbelievers at death, immediately and eternally (Matt. 25:46; Luke 16:23-24).

Our initial question early in this chapter can now be answered — namely, *when* do Christians go to heaven? Were Christians like John Bradford and Billy Bray correct in assuming that they would go immediately to heaven when they died? The Bible's answer is a positive 'Yes'. That the believer goes to heaven immediately at death is the consistent teaching of the Bible.

The psalmist says, 'You guide me with your counsel, and afterwards you will take me into glory' (Ps. 73:24).

As Stephen was being stoned to death he told his Jewish persecutors, 'Look ... I see heaven open and the Son of Man standing at the right hand of God' (Acts 7:56). His last words were, 'Lord Jesus, receive my spirit' (v. 59).

The apostle Paul looked forward to dying in order to 'be with Christ' in heaven, 'which is better by far' (Phil. 1:23). Earlier, the same apostle told the Corinthian Christians, 'We ... would prefer to be away from the body and at home with the Lord' (2 Cor. 5:8).

One of the two criminals crucified at the same time as Jesus Christ requested, 'Jesus, remember me when you come into your kingdom.' The Lord Jesus answered him quickly: 'Today you will be with me in paradise' (Luke 23:42,43). Notice the promise made here by Jesus Christ; the criminal is promised that he 'will be with me', that is, in Christ's immediate presence in paradise.

From other New Testament references we can see that the words 'heaven' and 'paradise' refer to the same place. If you compare, for example, the phrase 'the third heaven' in 2 Corinthians 12:2 with 'paradise' in verse 4 you can see that the same place, heaven, is being referred to. Again, we are told of 'the tree of life, which is in the paradise of God' (Rev. 2:7) but later in Revelation this same 'tree of life' is identified with 'the holy city' (22:14,19), which is heaven (see 21:1-2).

'Soul sleep'

Perhaps there may be one question still left unanswered in the minds of some readers concerning when the Christian goes to heaven. Does not the apostle Paul speak of 'soul sleep' in 1 Thessalonians 4:13,15? In other words, does this mean, for Christians who die before the Second Coming of Christ, that they are in some kind of unconscious state until the time of their resurrection? The apostle's words are: 'Brothers, we do not want you to be ignorant about those who fall asleep... We tell you that we who are still alive, who are left till the coming of the Lord, will certainly not precede those who have fallen asleep.'

The words of the same apostle in Philippians 1:23 make the theory of soul sleep for Christians untenable, for Paul there looks forward to being 'with Christ, which is better by far'. For the apostle, death would lead him into the immediate presence of Christ, not into some vague, unconscious state. Why then does he use the word 'sleep' to describe Christians who have died? Lloyd-Jones answers the question helpfully for us: 'It is a term which is used to describe an incomplete condition, an intermediate state. At the final "glorification", when the resurrection of the body takes place and man is fully saved in every respect, it will no longer be incomplete but full and complete. There is a sense in which that cannot happen until the glorification of the body. The body at death as it were "falls on sleep"; it is not yet revived and alive and active. So I take it that "sleep" refers mainly to the condition of the body. The body is asleep, waiting. It is no longer active, as it will be in the state of glorification; there is an intermediate condition.'[3]

The Bible teaching is clear and emphatic. At death, the Christian goes to be with the Lord in heaven — immediately. A seventeenth-century Puritan minister, John Flavel, captured

something of the wonder of this remarkable truth in one of his
sermons: 'To be lifted from a bed of sickness to a throne of
glory! To leave a sinful troublesome world, a sick and pained
body and be in a moment perfectly cured and feel yourself
perfectly well and free from all troubles... You cannot imagine what this will be like.'[4]

15.
Heaven: does everybody go there?

This is a question on the lips of many people. And it is not an idle question. Usually, it is posed out of concern for the welfare of other people, especially those who are not Christians and who may belong to one of the other world religions, such as Islam or Hinduism. It is a sensitive question, especially in view of the fact that Christians represent such a small percentage of the world's population. Are other people excluded from heaven? Is not God's purpose universal in its scope? In tackling these crucial questions, it is necessary to refer to the contemporary debate about universalism and religious pluralism.

Universalism

There is an important sense in which God's saving purposes in Christ have a worldwide dimension because people from all nations and cultures are invited and called to embrace Jesus Christ as Saviour and Lord. The invitation is extended to everyone, irrespective of where they live, their religion or their past behaviour. All are welcomed into the kingdom of the Lord Jesus Christ, Jews or Gentiles, rich or poor, young or old (Rom. 10:12-13; 11:11-25; Gal. 3:28). The good news is that heaven will be populated by believing sinners from all nations (Rev. 5:9-10).

However, the term 'universalism' is also used in a radically different way to refer to the belief or hope that the whole of humanity will be saved eventually, if not immediately, and irrespective of belief or religion. There are many variations of the theory and its history is 'a complex one'.[1] I only intend to refer to three types of contemporary universalism in order to sample the debate and feel the challenge of what is being written. The three types of contemporary universalism I want to sample are, first, what I call 'liberal' universalism; secondly, 'radical' universalism; and thirdly, 'evangelical' universalism. These types are different in their arguments and presuppositions but agree in their conclusion that everyone will eventually be saved and go to heaven.

Liberal universalism

Vatican II (1962-1965) marked a major change by the Roman Catholic Church towards its traditional dogma that there is 'no salvation outside the church'. The council affirmed that whatever was pure and true in other religions reflected 'a ray of that Truth which enlightens all men'.[2] Later, the papal encyclical *Redemptor Hominis* by Pope John Paul II in March 1979 insisted that redemption has been accomplished for all people because the whole of mankind is united with Christ and redeemed by virtue of the incarnation. On the Protestant side, Karl Barth's theology continued to exercise a powerful influence in the 1960s and early 1970s, particularly in relation to scholars like William Barclay, W. A. Visser't Hooft (World Council of Churches), T. F. Torrance and Leslie Newbigin. For example, Barclay later embraced universalism because of the fatherhood of God and the Christological orientation of divine love which embraces the whole of mankind. Newbigin adopts a similar approach.[3] On the Roman Catholic side, scholars like Raymond Panniker, Karl Rahner and Hans Küng adopted distinctive approaches to universalism in which Christ, in subtle ways, was regarded as central. Rahner, for example, regarded members of extra-Christian religions as *anonymous Christians*, having an implicit faith but unaware that it is related to Christ.[4] Küng distinguished between the 'general ... *ordinary*' way of salvation in other religions and the '*extraordinary*' way of salvation in the church.[5] However it may be expressed and argued, all these writers believe that all mankind will go to heaven.

Radical universalism

A strong case can be made for including writers like Rahner and Küng in this category but I have decided otherwise in order to show the even more radical contribution of John Hick who adopts what I call a relative 'God-centred' rather than a Christological approach. Hick is a prolific writer[6] in the area of religious pluralism. He argues that Christians must uphold the ultimate salvation of all God's creatures and then proceeds to reject Christ's deity and unique death as well as the Bible. His basic thesis is that there is one transcendent God common to all religions so that the universe of faiths must centre upon God, not upon Christianity or any other religion.

I have criticized both forms of universalism in detail elsewhere[7] and restrict myself here to the following observation. Hick adopts a reductionist methodology by means of which he relativizes biblical revelation and dogma, removing all the unique and distinctive tenets of Christianity. This methodology is an expression of Hick's liberal, critical approach to Scripture and dogma as well as his rationalist presuppositions.

Evangelical universalism

Recently a more 'evangelical' version of universalism has been popularized especially through the writings of Clark Pinnock[8] and John Sanders[9] in the United States of America. You need to understand from the outset that this position is very different from that of liberal and radical universalism. For one thing, Pinnock and Sanders claim to be evangelicals and committed to the inspiration of the Bible. They both reject liberalism in theology as well as the anti-supernatural presuppositions of Hick. Secondly, both authors insist on the uniqueness and finality of Jesus Christ in a world of different, conflicting religions. Thirdly, Pinnock and Sanders are eager to face up to the major challenge of religious pluralism and interact with its advocates.

And yet the fact that Pinnock and Sanders are evangelicals but at the same time espousing universalism is extremely disturbing. Pinnock's book has been described as 'a ground-breaking book that suggests some new possibilities of interpretation around the challenge of religious pluralism'.[10] We are also informed that 'Sanders has written a landmark work on the question of the ultimate destiny of those who do not hear the gospel in their lifetime.'[11]

Sanders, for example, believes that salvation is only found in Jesus Christ but he then refuses to accept the twin fact that the unevangelized are lost and also condemned to hell unless they trust in Christ. He writes concerning John 14:6 and Acts 4:12: 'They simply say there is no other way to heaven except through the work of Christ; they do not say one has to know about that work in order to benefit from that work.'[12] Hywel Jones rightly criticizes Sanders. He reminds us that the two parts of Acts 4:12 are linked by the preposition 'for', meaning 'because'. Peter is therefore insisting in this important statement that "There was salvation in no one else *because* [for] no one else has been given by heaven [God] to human beings as Saviour.'[13] And the negation, adds Jones, 'is itself deduced from the statement which precedes it'(v. 11), which is a quotation from Psalm 118. Clearly there is an 'exclusiveness' emphasized in Acts 4:12; salvation is found *only* in Jesus Christ and this has worldwide application. But faith in Christ is also necessary in order to receive Christ's salvation and the context in Acts 3:16,19 and 4:4 stresses the fact that the objective work of Christ's redemption must be appropriated personally in faith by individuals. Only such individuals go to heaven.

One of Pinnock's arguments, possibly 'the cornerstone of his argument',[14] is the attempt to show that 'pagan saints' in the Old and New Testaments like Melchizedek, Abimelech, Jethro, Rahab, Naaman and Cornelius received salvation through their own religions.[15] It can be shown conclusively[16] that such people in different contexts were privileged to receive special and saving revelation. The pagan Rahab became a believer in a most remarkable way while Jethro, Ruth and Naaman also became believers in Yahweh. They were not pagan 'believers' finding their way to heaven through their pagan religions with the help of general revelation.

Conclusion

It is now time for us to gather the threads together after sampling three different expressions of universalism. To the question, 'Does everyone go to heaven?', these universalists in their distinctive ways all answer positively in favour of what is called in theology a 'wider hope' or 'inclusivism'. Already, we have suggested that their understanding of key texts is flawed and that their presuppositions need to be challenged. In conclusion, a summary of the Bible teaching is given for your attention:

All who go to heaven, the elect, have been chosen
sovereignly by God the Father — Eph. 1:4; Matt.
25:34.

All are without excuse, whether they have heard the
gospel or not — Rom. 1:20.

All have sinned — Rom. 3:23.

All are condemned in Adam — Rom. 5:12-19.

All are guilty — Rom. 3:19-20.

All will be judged — Rom. 2:15-16.

All are invited to believe on Christ — John 3:16

All must call on the name of the Lord to be saved —
Rom. 10:11-13.

All who go to heaven have believed on the Lord Jesus
— John 3:18.

All the elect will reach heaven and no one chosen by
God will be lost — John 17:12,24.

Section III
What heaven is like

16.
Worth climbing?

Scafell Pike in Cumbria, at 3,210 feet, is the highest mountain
in England and it is situated in an attractive, popular area of
the country. One of the best routes to the summit of Scafell
Pike is from Seathwaite, the wettest inhabited place in England in terms of rainfall, averaging approximately 130 inches a
year. If you intend to climb the mountain then you are advised
to start early in the morning, choose a clear day and ensure
that you are well equipped. The climb itself is demanding but
there are some superb scenes on the way and delightful places
to view. For example, after struggling to climb up and then
out of Grains Gill, one can walk along the Wasdale path to
Sprinkling Tarn, which an experienced fell-walker in the area
describes as 'a most attractive sheet of water with an indented
rocky shore, its scenic quality enhanced by the massive cliffs
of Great End nearby and soaring above ... a delightful place'.[1]
Later on the climb, the same fell-walker urges walkers to take
a worthwhile digression of one mile to the top of Great End
which stands at 2,984 feet. Here 'A superb retrospective view
of Borrowdale unfolds' and looking down from the cliff edges
the impressive gullies are 'certainly quite thrilling'.[2]
   When one eventually reaches the mountain's summit, what
does one see? Is the effort to struggle up the mountain for
three hours or more rewarded by beautiful scenery and breathtaking views? Let Wainwright the fell-walker tell us in his own

words: 'Nature's design for the roof of England is a desolation of stones of all shapes and sizes, a barren waste where
only mosses and lichens can find sustenance, an inhospitable
desert without grace, without charm and without colour other
than the drab grey of volcanic rocks. Man's contribution to
the scene is a huge circular stone platform, a plaque com-
memorating the gift of the summit to the nation; an Ordnance
column, and litter. There is no beauty here.'[3]

A disappointment? Certainly a sense of ordinariness and
colourless desolation awaits climbers as they view the summit
itself. But that is not the end of the story. In a later book,
Wainwright provides us with a further, complementary perspective on the Scafell Pike summit. While the summit itself is
ordinary, nevertheless, Wainwright claims, 'This is a very
special place, and there is no other like it.' In addition to the
challenge, enjoyment and significance of climbing England's
highest mountain, Wainwright explains that the ultimate reason for his claim is that the summit provides 'the most far-
reaching panorama' in England. He adds, 'All the major heights
in Lakeland are in display in a view crowded with detail and
extending across the Irish Sea to the Isle of Man and, on rare
occasions, to the mountains of Snowdonia in North Wales,
the Mountains of Mourne in Ireland and the Galloway Hills in
Scotland.'[4] A magnificent panorama indeed!

The Christian is a pilgrim travelling to his home in heaven.
However, the journey to heaven is a climb; in the words of
Jonathan Edwards, it is 'uphill' all the way. On this 'uphill'
climb, Christians have to travel hard and long each day, preparing for death, growing in holiness, thus 'coming nearer and
nearer to heaven'.[5] Paul, the apostle, uses the picture of an
athlete in Philippians 3:11-16 to express the way in which he
struggled against sin, the world and the devil, and 'pressed
on' purposely by God's grace towards glory and the resurrection. In a very graphic way he describes an athlete straining

every muscle and nerve in order to reach the finishing line as well as the prize. But what does the Christian see and experience at the end of the uphill climb and race?

It will certainly not be an anti-climax; of that we can be sure. Heaven will be fantastic, breathtakingly beautiful, thrilling, deeply satisfying and perfect. And the main reason for this is that Christians will there see and enjoy their Saviour, the Lord Jesus Christ, in all his radiance and beauty. In fact, heaven is so glorious that words fail us here, and even in heaven, to express adequately its beauty and glories. That is what the hymn-writer, Bernard of Cluny, expressed in the twelfth century:

Jerusalem the golden,
With milk and honey blest,
Beneath thy contemplation
Sink heart and voice oppressed:
I know not, O I know not
What joys await us there,
What radiancy of glory,
What bliss beyond compare.

Many other Christians too, including preachers, have found it impossible to describe the bliss and privileges of heaven. For example, Jonathan Edwards (1703-1758) was a famous American preacher and theologian. Despite his considerable intellectual abilities, deep experiences of God and profound understanding of Christian doctrines, yet he felt unable to express the outstanding attractions and splendour of heaven for Christians. From the text of Revelation 21:18, he concluded that 'There is nothing upon earth that will suffice to represent to us the glory of heaven.'[6] The Welsh eighteenth-century hymn-writer, William Williams, knew that his skill with words and the telescope of his imagination were inadequate instruments to convey the matchless beauties and joys of heaven; he finds himself too far away from heaven to see as clearly as he wants:

The lenses lack the power, the distance is too vast.
I comprehend but dimly the glorious life to last.

Williams recognized his inability to describe the loveliness of heaven: 'It is impossible to portray the glory of heaven,' he writes, 'and to describe fully the bliss to be experienced there.'[7] He was under no illusion. Nothing he said in his hymns or poems about heaven could convey 'a thousandth part of the majesty and the splendour within' that place. In an imaginary letter of 1769, he affirms that the riches and the unsurpassing beauty of heaven are inexpressible in any language and nothing in this world is worthy of being compared with heaven. The contrast is too great and heaven itself too glorious. And this point is confirmed in the New Testament by the apostle Paul:

However, as it is written:

'No eye has seen,
    no ear has heard,
no mind has conceived
    what God has prepared for those who love him'
                                              (1 Cor. 2:9).

Another eighteenth-century Welsh poet, John Thomas, underlines the same point in one of his poems:

No one ever saw and no ear ever heard
What Jesus has got for his children prepared;
No heart can imagine the pleasure sublime
Of bliss everlasting in a hundred years' time.[8]

And yet in the Bible God himself does describe heaven for us, but usually in picture language and by means of contrasts, images and metaphors which all highlight the sublime and transcendent glories of heaven.

In this third section of the book, several of these divinely given picture descriptions of heaven will be used and explained simply. My purpose in doing this is to try, however feebly, to indicate what a wonderful place heaven really is and to explain why Christians will be so happy there.

17.
Heaven: our home

As I write this chapter, it is exactly a week before Christmas Day. Although there are sad memories yet Christmas is also a happy family occasion for us. One reason is that our children are returning home from university where they are students. They too have been looking forward to coming home. It will be great to be together again as a family and enjoy each other's company. Another reason is that my mother will also join us for about ten days and we shall see other close relatives. Home: for a lot of people, but sadly not for all, the word means the place where we are loved, cared for, welcomed and wanted. It is also the place where we can relax and just be ourselves.

A competent New Testament scholar claims that, for the Lord Jesus, the 'primary idea of heaven for believers is that of an eternal home'.[1] His claim may well be justified especially in view of the famous statement by the Lord in John 14:2: 'In my Father's house are many rooms; if it were not so, I would have told you. I am going there to prepare a place for you.'

These words demand careful attention from us. One reason for this is that this verse is the most specific and detailed statement on heaven recorded in the Gospel of John. And it is possibly the most detailed description of heaven given by the Lord Jesus Christ in any of the four Gospels. Another reason for its importance is the richness and variety of teaching contained within the verse. It is all too easy to read these words quickly and superficially and so to miss out on the profound teaching which lies under the surface. The Lord's statement in John 14:2 will be approached in two ways, namely, in terms of its context and comfort.

The context of the Lord's words

A golden rule in interpreting Scripture is that an individual text like John 14:2 should always be considered and understood in the light of its context, that is, in the context of the preceding verses and chapter, or even chapters. For our purposes, we need to remember two parallel themes in the immediate context.

1. His approaching death

First, and most important of all, the Lord Jesus was fast approaching his death on the cross. That was the reason why he had come into the world; he came to save his people. On many earlier occasions even in John's Gospel he had spoken about his unique death,[2] but now it was almost upon him. In fact, he was only a matter of a day or so away from dying on the cross. And he knew what to expect and realized the agonies of his impending sacrifice. It was not an appealing or comfortable prospect; rather it filled him with alarm and sorrow. He acknowledged in prayer: 'Now my heart is troubled, and what shall I say? "Father, save me from this hour"? No, it was for this very reason I came to this hour...' (12:27).

His impending death, therefore, loomed large in his own thoughts and plans. And it was time to tell the disciples more about this death.

2. The confusion of the disciples

The second parallel theme in the immediate context is the alarm
and confusion felt by the disciples on hearing from the Lord
Jesus that he was going to die. They could not understand,
nor could they accept the fact, that Jesus would die. Notice
how towards the end of chapter 13 the Lord spells out some
of the implications of his departure (vv. 33,36). But there was
also another problem for them. Not only was the Lord Jesus
about to leave them, but Peter was going to let Jesus down.
Would the other disciples be just as fickle and unreliable? At
this point, they were all deeply upset and feared they might be
on the verge of a major disaster.

It is for this reason that the Lord begins chapter 14 with
what are probably two commands in verse 1: 'Trust in God;
trust also in me.' These two commands at least imply the deity
of Christ and his equality with the Father. The commands are
given because the disciples are 'troubled' in heart. Interestingly, this is the same word which the Lord uses of himself
(12:27; 13:21) yet he is more concerned here with the disciples than with himself. In verse 2 he goes on to explain why
they should trust him. Here then is the context of the verse.

The comfort in the promise

Make no mistake about it. The words of verses 2 to 4 are
intended to comfort and encourage these troubled disciples.
What then is the comfort of verse 2? This can be described in
five ways:

1. The Lord is talking about heaven

The 'simplest explanation is the best', writes Don Carson,[3]
that the 'Father's house' refers to heaven. With equal clarity

and insistence, William Hendriksen claims that 'The Father's house is heaven.'[4] Professor R. V. G. Tasker similarly writes that 'The thought here is that there are many dwelling-places in heaven' and that it is 'a permanent home'.[5] The eminent Scottish minister John Brown, who studied the Gospels for more than forty years, wrote, 'There is little doubt that, by the house of our Lord's Father, we are to understand heaven…'[6] Bishop J. C. Ryle gives his endorsement to this interpretation: 'Heaven is a place of "mansions" of lasting, permanent and eternal dwellings…'[7] What a comfort for Christians!

Heaven is home for Christians

'My Father's house' is a phrase pregnant with meaning. It illustrates, for example, Christ's complete familiarity with heaven. He knows all about it, for it is his eternal home. For Christ, heaven is the real and abiding world. But there is more. It is, says Christ, 'my Father's house'. Yes, it is figurative language and John Brown suggests it brings to mind the image of a magnificent palace which the Great King has built.[8] Just as the temple in Jerusalem was the symbol of God's presence, so heaven is God's house because there the most glorious revelation is made of his character and Christians there enjoy intimate, uninterrupted fellowship with him.

Two different but figurative Greek words are used in this second verse to describe heaven. One is the word translated 'house' and the other is translated usually as either 'mansions' (AV), 'rooms' (NIV) or 'dwelling-places' (NASB). The Greek *oikos* translates literally as 'house' but, of course, there is a world of difference between a house and a home. Allow me to illustrate this difference from my own experience. Because of the nature of my father's employment, it was necessary for him to relocate our family on several occasions. I was too young to remember the first two houses we lived in and we were only in them for a short period of time. However, I remember clearly the small terraced house we occupied in north-east Wales near the border with England. Later, when I was a teenager, we moved as a family to an industrial area some forty miles away and I lived there for about eleven years. Although I had lived in different houses, my home was always where my parents lived at the time. It was my family that made a house into a home for me. The same was true after I married. My wife and I are now living in our fourth house but each house was our home while we lived there.

The point is that heaven is our home, not merely a house. This fact is strengthened by the second Greek word, *mone,* translated as 'mansions', 'dwelling-places' or 'rooms'. The word occurs only twice in the New Testament, both times in John 14. It is in verse 23 where the same word is used the second time, but this time in relation to God the Father and Son: 'Jesus replied, "If anyone loves me, he will obey my teaching. My Father will love him, and we will come to him and make our *home* with him" ' (italics mine). The Christian who loves and obeys Christ enjoys a richer and more mature fellowship with the Lord here and now because the Father and Son have made their abode or home with him. Similarly, according to John 14:2, the Lord informs his worried disciples that he has gone in order to prepare a home for them in which their relationship to him will be perfected.

The same point is made, but in a different way, by Bishop Handley Moule as he reflects on the words of Paul when he speaks of being 'at home with the Lord' in 2 Corinthians 5:6-9: 'The Heaven beyond death is Home. It is not only rest or refuge: it is nothing less than Home... The Home will be indeed a circle of blessed fellowship, a place of inconceivable interchange of love and joy among its inhabitants. But the supreme bliss of it which will always spring up through everything else, and be first in everything, is this — we shall have "got Home to the Lord".'[9]

We will continue this subject in the next chapter.

18.
Heaven: our Father's home

As we continue the theme of heaven as our home, we need to remind ourselves of the main points already established in the last chapter. With regard to the Lord's important words in John 14:2, we considered first the *context* and saw that two parallel themes are interwoven in the preceding and later verses: the Lord Jesus' deep awareness of *his imminent death*; and *the alarm felt by the disciples* on hearing from their Lord that he was going to die — and soon.

Secondly, we emphasized the *comfort* to be found in these words. We saw that the words of verses 2-4 are intended to comfort and encourage the troubled, frightened disciples. From verse 2, this comfort can be described in five ways. Two of them we considered in the previous chapter: first, the fact that the Lord Jesus talks about *heaven*, and second, that heaven is *home* for Christians. We now proceed in this chapter with other aspects of this comfort from John 14:2.

Heaven is our Father's home

Heaven belongs to God the Father as well as to the Son and the Holy Spirit. The emphasis of Jesus Christ in John 14:2 is that heaven is his 'Father's home'; it belongs to him.

This aspect of heaven is profoundly important and significant. It is in Matthew's Gospel, more than anywhere else in the New Testament, that we find the phrase 'Father in heaven' used; it occurs in Matthew about ten times, whereas it occurs only once each in the Gospels of Mark and Luke. Interestingly, half of the references in Matthew are found in the Sermon on the Mount in chapters 5-7 and these all add a tender and personal touch by describing God as 'your' Father in heaven. Three times also in chapters 5-7 the term 'heavenly Father' is employed, each time again prefaced by the word 'your'. Not only is God the Father in heaven; he is also 'your' Father and he is in an intimate, loving relationship with all Christians.

Briefly, the title 'Father' in relation to God is used in the Bible in three important ways:

1. an exclusive *trinitarian* fatherhood which is unique in relation to God the Son;

2. a *universal* fatherhood with regard to all people in virtue of his relation to them as their creator, preserver and ruler (see, e.g., Acts 17:25-29; James 1:18; Mal. 2:10);

3. a *redemptive* fatherhood which applies only to those redeemed by Christ; these, and these alone, are adopted as sons and daughters into God's family.

Consider the following Bible statement underlining this fact: 'But when the time had fully come, God sent his Son, born of a woman, born under the law, to redeem those under law, that we might receive the full rights of sons. Because you are sons, God sent the Spirit of his Son into our hearts, the Spirit who calls out, "*Abba*, Father" ' (Gal. 4:4-6; see also 1 John 3:1-3).

The First Person in the Godhead is not only, in the words of the apostle Paul, 'the God and Father of our Lord Jesus

Christ' (Eph. 1:3), but he is also the God and Father of all who believe in Jesus Christ. When Christians go to heaven, therefore, they go to the home of their heavenly Father, the one who loves them and has shown such infinite care towards them on earth. In a very real sense, they are children going home to see and to be with their wonderful Father.

Heaven has sufficient room for all Christians

Here is the clear emphasis in the Lord's words, 'In my Father's house are *many rooms...*' (italics mine); it is the idea of ample room and provision for all Christians. Before elaborating on this, it is necessary to warn of three *wrong* interpretations of the phrase 'many rooms'.

First, the phrase does *not* refer to 'stations' or 'temporary lodgings'. On the basis of the way this phrase is rendered in the old Latin Vulgate translation and by the early scholar Origen and, more recently, by Westcott and Temple, some have thought that the phrase 'many mansions' pictures heaven as an ongoing journey with several temporary stops for rest until eventually the destination is reached. But this is wild imagination rather than exposition of the text and context. We have already noted that the word translated 'rooms' or 'mansions' has the idea of permanent residence rather than perpetual movement or progress. The 'Father's house' is our final destination — heaven.

Nor, secondly, do the expressions 'Father's house' and 'many rooms' refer to the church as a spiritual house.[1]

Nor, thirdly, is Jonathan Edwards justified in suggesting that 'many rooms' describes the different accommodation and degrees of reward given to believers.[2]

'The thought here' in John 14:2, argues Professor Tasker, 'is that there are many dwelling places in heaven, where there is room enough for all believers.'[3] Carson confirms this interpretation, namely, that ample provision is made and enough space is available for the disciples and all other believers.[4]

On several occasions I have known the experience of being told that a train or aeroplane flight was full. One incident that I remember vividly took place in Korea, where my colleague, the Rev. Jong Tae Lee, and I tried to book seats on an express train from Seoul to Kwang-ju in the south-west of the country. The response was disappointing. Each train that day was fully booked and there was no room for us. What about flying? It was the same story: 'Sorry, all our flights are fully booked.' Eventually we succeeded in obtaining a couple of seats on a coach although it increased our journey time to well over five hours. On another occasion, this time at home, it was the experience of trying to buy tickets for the famous Cardiff Young Singer of the World Competition. We found, to our disappointment, that all the tickets had been sold and there was no more room.

For real Christians, however, there will always be room in heaven. No Christian will be left outside, even though the number of Christians worldwide is increasing each year. In Asia alone it is estimated that approximately 67,000 people become Christians each day, while 150 new churches are planted each day in Africa. The number of Protestant Christians in Latin America has soared from 50,000 in 1900 to over five million in 1950 then fifty million in 1990. And the number could be as high as 137 million by the beginning of the next millennium. But there are many more people yet to be saved, including those in Israel and a greater number of Gentiles (Rom. 11:12-26). Great crowds of believers will yet throng into heaven but, adds the Lord Jesus in John 14:2, there is ample room for all. No believer will be shut out of heaven; young and old, weak and strong, insignificant as well as famous Christians will all be welcomed into the mansions of heaven.

Heaven is a prepared home for Christians

In order to banish any fears or doubts we may have, the Lord Jesus reassures us that he himself has personally prepared heaven for his people: 'I am going there to prepare a place for you.' As Carson observes, this statement presupposes that the 'place' existed before Jesus went there. He did not arrive there after his ascension and then frantically begin to search for heaven. No, he is familiar with heaven and has prepared it for us. In the context of the theology of John's Gospel, it is his going via the cross, his resurrection and ascension which prepares heaven for us. He opens heaven to us; we are loved, known and cared for, and even expected, in heaven. Yes, heaven has been wonderfully prepared by the Lord Jesus.

Commenting on the Lord's words in John 14:3, 'I will come back and take you to *be with me...*' (italics mine), Hendriksen writes, 'Christ's loving presence will be that which makes the Father's house a real home and a real heaven for the children of God. Wherever Jesus is, there, too, will his disciples be.'[5]

Heaven will be home for the Christian. In the next chapters we will see just how wonderful that home is.

19.
Heaven: with the Lord

The more biblical way of describing the destiny of Christians when they die is that they have gone to be 'with the Lord'. Nowhere does the New Testament actually speak of Christians 'going to heaven'; rather, they are 'with the Lord'. And 'here', writes Thomas Boston, 'lies the chief happiness of the saints in heaven...'[1] That is not an exaggeration either; it will be our greatest happiness to be 'with the Lord'. Perhaps you are not convinced. Or maybe you have not thought about it before and find it difficult to appreciate. In this chapter we are going to consider what it means to be 'with the Lord'. First of all, we will underline some of the important Bible references where this phrase occurs and, secondly, but more briefly, we will attempt to appreciate the significance and thrill for Christians of being 'with the Lord'.

Bible references

'Jesus answered him, "I tell you the truth, today you will be with me in paradise"' (Luke 23:43).

It was an awful moment. Three men were nailed to separate wooden crosses and within another three hours one of them,

Jesus, would be dead. Two of these men were criminals and deserved to be punished. The person in the centre, however, was different; in fact, he was very different indeed. This man had not broken any law; on the contrary, he had devoted himself to healing, teaching and helping people. He was Jesus Christ, the Son of God, and, of course, he was dying on behalf of others in order to save them. His was a unique and substitutionary death.

But notice what happened on this occasion. One of the criminals hurled insults at Jesus: 'Aren't you the Christ?' he asked. 'Save yourself and us!' (Luke 23:39). His friend and partner in crime intervened and rebuked him, insisting that they themselves were guilty and were being 'punished justly' whereas Jesus Christ 'has done nothing wrong' (v. 41). Then immediately he addressed a personal request to the Lord: 'Jesus, remember me when you come into your kingdom.' It was obvious that this criminal now had a change of heart. His request was an expression of his personal repentance and faith in Jesus Christ. He was really a new man. The answer he received must have been an enormous comfort and thrill to him as he approached death. 'Today', he heard Jesus say to him, 'you will be with me in paradise.'

Can you imagine the man's surprise? He asked only for a blessing in the distant future at the end of the world, but he is told that on that very day he dies he will be with Christ in 'paradise'. Again, whereas the man only asked to be remembered, now he is told by Jesus, 'You will be with me.' And what about 'paradise'? What does it refer to? The words 'paradise' and 'heaven' are interchangeable and refer to the same place.[2] Within hours, Jesus assured the dying but believing criminal, he would be in heaven 'with me'. A glorious prospect indeed!

*'Father, I want those you have given me to be with me where
I am, and to see my glory...'* (John 17:24).

These words were spoken in prayer by the Lord Jesus to God
the Father. The whole chapter here records an important and
moving prayer which Jesus prayed for his disciples initially
(John 17:6-19) and then for all who would believe on him in
the future (vv. 20-26). As J. C. Ryle indicates, the words of
verse 24 are 'a singularly beautiful and touching conclusion to
our Lord's remarkable prayer'.[3] Our Lord Jesus makes several requests for Christians in this great prayer, but especially
in this section he prays for our spiritual and visible unity in this
world.

    Then, in verse 24, he expresses his desire that all Christians
'be with me where I am'. Although we love Christ yet in this
world we only read and hear of Christ and long for him, but
when we die then we shall be with him. 'We need no more
information,' adds J. C. Ryle. 'Where that blessed person is
who was born for us, died for us and rose again, there can be
no lack of anything.'[4] And even more remarkably still, our
Lord's desire is that his people may 'be constantly with me
where I am'.[5] Yes, it will be a permanent enjoyment of Christ's
immediate presence.

*'We are confident, I say, and would prefer to be away from
the body and at home with the Lord'* (2 Cor. 5:8).

Notice that last phrase in the statement, namely, 'with the Lord',
for it is all-important and the perspective is also challenging.
For example, have you been made more aware of your physical frailty? Do you only have a short period of time in which to
live? Or are you afraid of death, or concerned for someone
you love who is dying? Well, listen to the words of the apostle
Paul: 'Therefore we do not lose heart' (2 Cor. 4:16). He said
this even though his own body was 'wasting away'. Why was

he not depressed and in the depths of despair? He tells us the secret. He experiences daily, spiritual renewal (v. 17) and he is sure that ahead of him awaits an 'eternal glory'. In the following chapter he explains what this 'eternal glory' is. Although he will die physically, yet he will go to heaven immediately; later, his body will be raised from the grave. The future is a wonderful one indeed and not even death can frighten the apostle Paul. Actually, he would 'prefer to be away from the body', that is, to die (2 Cor. 5:8).Why? Not in order to escape from problems and responsibilities, but in order to be 'at home with the Lord'. For the Christian, heaven is to be with Christ and physical death leads immediately to heaven. That really is exciting.

'I am torn between the two: I desire to depart and be with Christ, which is better by far' (Phil. 1:23).

This was no exaggeration on Paul's part; he really meant it. He knew that the many young churches which had been established by him and his colleagues still needed his leadership and he was prepared to stay in order to help them a little longer. On the other hand, Paul had a deep longing 'to depart' and die in order to 'be with Christ, which is better by far'. As one writer expresses it, 'The apostle knows that when his soul departs from this earthly life, it is immediately *with Christ*. It does not "go out of existence" until the day of the resurrection, nor does it "go to sleep"... It at once enjoys blessed fellowship with the Saviour. That is "very far better" than to remain in the flesh.'[6]

'And so we will be with the Lord for ever' (1 Thess. 4:17).

In this familiar section, the writer describes some of the things which will occur when the Lord Jesus returns to this world as King and Judge. Christians who have died will accompany

Jesus Christ on his return; their bodies will first be raised and then those Christians who are still living in this world at the time will 'meet the Lord in the air'. The description here is almost breathtaking. But notice what the climax is: 'We will be *with the Lord* for ever.' Possibly there are many more details we would like to receive concerning these facts but, writes Leon Morris, 'When Paul comes to that great fact [that 'we will be with the Lord for ever'], which includes everything else, and makes everything else unimportant, he ceases. There is nothing to add to it.'[7] And that will be the full realization of God's covenant promises, the central message of which is that God 'will live with them. They will be his people, and God himself will be with them and be their God' (Rev. 21:3).

What does it mean to be 'with the Lord'?

In answering this question we need to start from basics and recap a little. In the first place, we need to remember that God is everywhere present in this universe, so that it is impossible for us to go anywhere where he is not present. We call this God's *omnipresence*; because he is God, he is everywhere. It is a staggering thought, but then God is not confined like humans to one specific location.

But there is more. Christians know God's *gracious* presence with them all the time even though they are not always conscious of it. And God has promised to be with Christians in their daily lives in order to bless, guide and encourage them in living for him.

There are occasions, too, when we are more aware of the Lord's presence with us. 'But for Jesus and his presence', a Christian missionary by the name of John Paton testified years ago, 'I would have gone mad beside that lonely grave.' His wife had died in giving birth to their first child and now, seven days later, the baby had died and was being buried in the same grave. The Lord was with John Paton in his deep sorrow and loneliness. Or it may be in prayer or reading the Bible when a Christian senses that God is near. It is a comfort and joy to be with God in this way although the circumstances may at times be sad or difficult.

There are special times, particularly in periods of revival in churches, when God allows us to experience his *felt* presence in very powerful ways. And it can often be overwhelming and indescribable. Suddenly, God's presence becomes gloriously real, satisfying and joyful; it is his felt presence. For example, Ebenezer Morris, a preacher of the Calvinistic Methodist denomination in Wales early in the nineteenth century, preached on a memorable occasion on the words: 'Yet he has made with me an everlasting covenant, ordered in all things, and sure' (2 Sam. 23:5, AV). The preacher explained each word of the text clearly and powerfully. He pictured the covenant between God and sinners in Christ as a covenant of peace with the enemy, as a covenant of friendship and intimate relationship and also as a marriage covenant. While everything in the world changed, the preacher explained that God's covenant with his people was sure, unchangeable and eternal. As he continued to explain that God's mercy would never depart from them, it was too much for the congregation to bear. The presence of God overwhelmed them and the praise flowing from the great crowd of hearers was deafening but sincere and joyful. God's felt presence had been manifested under the preaching of the Word. And it has happened many times in the history of the church.

Even more wonderful however, is the *immediate* presence of God in heaven. A simple illustration may help at this point. When I am away from home, I am eager to talk to my family on the telephone. Although it is helpful and encouraging to talk yet I would prefer to be with them and see them. From overseas, I am sometimes able to send a fax and receive a faxed message with up-to-date news of my family. Again, this is thrilling but it is only a substitute for being with those I love. Similarly, this is true of our relationship as Christians with the Lord. We talk to the Lord in prayer and he speaks to us through the Bible and these lines of communication are essential and precious as well as encouraging for us. There is a sense too, in which the Lord is with us here, but in heaven it will be so much better. The distance between us and the veil dimming Christ's glory will be removed and we shall be with him and actually see him as he is. This is the theme of the next chapter but before closing this chapter I want to refer to Peter Morgan.

Peter and his wife, Jane, were students in my theological college and training for missionary work in Brazil. Jane finished studies earlier to have and care for their baby, Ceridwen, while Peter completed his studies successfully in June 1994. They intended going back to their home church in Reading for a year and then on to Brazil early in 1996 to be involved in Theological Education by Extension for church leaders. For several months in 1994 Peter was eager that he and other Christians should enter into the reality of what Paul was praying for when he pleaded with God '… that you may know him better … that you may know the hope to which he has called you … and his incomparably great power for us who believe…' (Eph. 1:17-21). On 18 September of that year, 1994, Peter died as the result of a tragic climbing accident the previous day. For Peter the prayer of Ephesians chapter 1 which he had prayed earnestly for months had now become a glorious reality. Peter is 'with the Lord'.

20.
Heaven: seeing the Lord

All Christians will see the Lord in heaven. Not one Christian will miss out on this supreme privilege. That is the clear, emphatic and exciting message of the Bible. And the Lord Jesus confirms the fact: 'Blessed are the pure in heart, for they will see God'(Matt. 5:8). Here is 'one of the greatest utterances to be found anywhere in the whole realm of Holy Scripture'.[1] There is, of course, a condition laid down. The promise applies only to those who are 'pure in heart'; that is, those whose hearts have been cleansed and their lives made holy by the Lord. On another occasion, shortly before his crucifixion, the Lord Jesus expressed this desire in his prayer: 'Father, I want those you have given me to be with me where I am, *and to see my glory...*' (John 17:24, italics mine). His desire is that all Christians will 'gaze for ever'[2] in heaven on our mediator in the splendour of his deity and his glorified human nature. There is no question of the Lord's desire not being fulfilled. One reason is that he no longer 'prays' here[3] but 'frankly expresses his will to the Father'[4] (the Greek translated in the NIV as 'I want' is literally 'I will') and his will is in perfect conformity to that of the Father. Christians, then, will definitely see Christ in his glory in heaven.

This fact is also underlined in other parts of the New Testament. For example, referring to the Lord Jesus Christ on his return in glory to this world, the apostle John declares, 'We

shall see him as he is' (1 John 3:2). Notice again that it is only
Christians who will see Christ in this way. The immediate context makes the point emphatically. In verse 1 we are informed
that 'the Father has lavished on us' his great love; here the
apostle is astonished at the amazing love of God which has
made us Christians and 'children of God'. Such Christians are
in stark contrast to 'the world' of unbelievers who do 'not
know' the Lord. From the perspective of the present, in which
we have been made the 'children of God', the apostle turns in
verse 2 to the future hope of Christians. Two brief but thrilling
points are made here.

First of all, 'We shall be like him.' Obviously this cannot
mean that Christians will become divine like the Lord Jesus.
Rather it means that they will one day be like the Lord Jesus in
terms of purity and holiness. And that is a staggering truth.
Both when Christians die and also at the time of the Lord's
return, the slow but progressive work of making them holy
will be complete. Yes, Christians will be as clean and holy as
the Lord Jesus himself. 'Heaven', John Owen rightly insists,
'is a state of deliverance from sin, from all sin, in all the causes,
concomitants and effects of it.'⁵ Isobel Kuhn refers to Christians who claim that the most wonderful thing of all in heaven
will be to see the Lord face to face. What she looked forward
to was 'to be with the Lord *with the root of sin gone*. To
fellowship with Him without the lazy flesh dragging us back,
or unwanted thoughts of pride and self constantly straining
us. To be finally rid of corruption, to worship and enjoy Him
with heart purged into His own purity, *that* will be an advance
over anything that is possible on earth.'⁶

The second thrilling point which the apostle John makes
briefly here is that 'We shall see him as he is.' We need to
pause here and explain in more detail the significance of these
glorious words.

There are different ways in which we can see the Lord here
and now. For one thing, the Lord is to be seen in *creation*.

'The heavens declare the glory of God; the skies proclaim the work of his hands' (Ps. 19:1). The Bible is even more precise on the point: 'For since the creation of the world God's invisible qualities — his eternal power and divine nature — have been clearly seen, being understood from what has been made, so that men are without excuse' (Rom. 1:20). The mountains and oceans, trees and vegetation all display God to us. Sadly, unbelievers resist this light, refusing to acknowledge God's glory and authority as Creator.

We can also see the Lord revealed in *the Bible*; here we can see much more of the Lord and read a great deal about his character and purposes. The Bible is often described as 'special revelation' for the reason that in it God has provided additional information concerning his plan to save people. And in so many ways we can see the Lord in this divine book.

Christians also see God at work in *history*; they can feel God is near to them and helping them. In the middle of all his difficulties, for example, Moses 'persevered because he saw him who is invisible' (Heb. 11:27). In other words, Moses was aware of the Lord, trusted in him and knew that he was in control even of difficult, impossible situations. Similarly, Christians can often see the Lord at work in their lives.

There is a sense too, in which Christians can see the Lord in the breaking of bread and taking of the wine; this is often referred to as *the Lord's Supper,* or Holy Communion. Baptism and the Lord's Supper are the two ordinances, or sacraments, appointed by the Lord Jesus for Christians to observe in his church. However, the public reading and preaching of the Bible are of primary importance and should always precede and dominate the ordinances of baptism and the Lord's Supper. 'Without the Word,' declared John Calvin, 'the sacrament is but a dumb show; the Word must go before.'[7] But why add these two ordinances if the Bible is so important? The Lord has given the ordinances in order to help us appreciate biblical truths. The Word is addressed to our sense of hearing as well as to the mind and conscience, whereas the sense of sight is also involved in the Lord's Supper. The bread pictures the broken body of the Lord Jesus on the cross dying for our sin, while the wine pictures his blood and life given freely on our behalf. Quite often in the Lord's Supper we can see the Lord in a moving way as we eat the bread and drink the wine in memory of him and his sacrifice.

Although we see the Lord in all these related ways, but especially in the Bible, in heaven we shall see him in a direct and more glorious way. 'Now we see but a poor reflection,' the apostle Paul reminds us. 'Then we shall see face to face' (1 Cor. 13:12). And that is what the apostle John underlines: 'We shall see him as he is.'

In the context of higher education, I have been privileged to meet a number of famous individuals. I had heard and read about them before and seen some of them on TV news or current affairs programmes. To see them in person, however, and face to face was considerably better than reading about them or seeing them on TV. Now this comparison is imperfect because the Lord Jesus is with Christians here in a vital way even though they only see him indirectly in the Bible. Christians enjoy intimate, spiritual fellowship with him and he is real to them. However, the point I want to draw from the comparison is that it will be even more wonderful for Christians to see the Lord face to face. But notice that 'We shall see him *as he is*', not as a baby in Bethlehem or being tempted in the desert, or praying intensely in Gethsemane. Nor shall we see him hanging on a cross with a crown of thorns on his head or being forsaken by his Father. How then will we see him? John replies, 'as he is', that is, in all his beauty and splendour as the returning King and exalted Lord.

There are three Greek words used in the New Testament to describe the return of the Lord Jesus. The word most often used is *parousia*, meaning both 'presence' and 'arrival'.

Apocalupsis is a second word and highlights the uncovering and revealing of what was to some extent previously concealed. The Lord of glory who is now exalted and rules from heaven will be revealed fully to all. The third Greek word used is *epiphaneia* and denotes that the Lord's arrival and unveiling will be indescribably glorious. The apostle Paul speaks of 'the splendour of his coming' (2 Thess. 2:8) and his 'glorious appearing' (Titus 2:13). Accompanied by angels and archangels, as well as Christians who have already died, he will come on the clouds of heaven as the King of kings and Lord of lords. As he places all enemies under his feet, all peoples everywhere will have to acknowledge that 'Jesus Christ is Lord' (Phil. 2:11).

Christians will see him in all this unrivalled splendour and as Saviour and Lord. For those Christians still alive on earth when Christ returns, faith will turn into sight and 'grace into glory'. No preachers will be required then, nor even a Bible; nor will Christians need to use bread and wine to remember his death, for they will see him 'as he is'. Only dimly can Christians see the Lord here on earth but they will see him directly, clearly and fully in the future.

Some questions can helpfully be posed at this point. How are the statements of Matthew 5:8 and 1 John 3:2 to be reconciled and understood? Is the seeing of God which is referred to in the beatitude different from the sight of the Lord Jesus in his mediatorial glory? Do we see God with the naked eye, or is it a spiritual insight and vision only? Over several centuries these questions have been discussed and debated by theologians. Like many others, Jonathan Edwards believed that 'The vision of God is the heaven of heaven,'[8] and that ultimate glory is not in seeing friends or relatives in heaven but God himself.[9] W. G. T. Shedd also 'infers that there will be a full and unclouded vision of God in the future life'.[10] He adds, 'This is one of those "eternal things" which are not seen as yet, but which will be seen hereafter.' This sight of God has often been described as 'the beatific vision'.

Thomas Boston had no doubt about it: 'The souls of the saints shall see God himself: so the scriptures teach us...'[11] and it will be a 'ravishing sight ... seeing the Father, the Son and the Holy Ghost, not with their bodily eyes ... but with the eyes of their understanding ... they shall see Him in the fulness of His glory ... eternally, without interruption, feast their eyes upon Him and be ever viewing His glorious perfections...'[12]

However, the Puritan John Owen cautions us: 'We can never have an immediate enjoyment of God in the immensity of his nature, nor can any created understanding conceive any such thing.'[13] Jonathan Edwards thinks the sight of God in heaven is 'rare'.[14]

The question as to whether Christians see God with the naked eye or with spiritual insight and vision only is for Dr Martyn Lloyd-Jones 'very difficult to understand. I do not intend to answer it... We just do not know.'[15] However, he concludes, 'All we know is that there is this glorious promise that, in some way or other, the pure in heart shall see God.'

John Owen agrees but warns, 'The infinite incomprehensible excellencies of the divine nature' are not the immediate object of our faith either here or in heaven. Rather, 'The manifestation of them in Christ is the immediate object of our faith here and ... of our sight hereafter...'[16] Owen is rightly emphatic: 'We look for no other heaven, we desire none...'

John Bunyan's Mr Stand-Fast, as he stood in the river of death, declared, 'I am going now to see that head that was crowned with thorns, and that face that was spit upon, for me. I have formerly lived by hearsay, and faith, but now I go where I shall live by sight, and shall be with him, in whose company I delight myself.'[17]

That is the hope which the apostle John holds out for Christians: 'We shall see him as he is.' Christians will behold his glorious body, which is personally united to his divine nature and exalted above all. They will see the head that had been crowned with thorns, as well as the hands and feet once nailed to the cross for the redemption of sinners. His glorified body will shine with unimaginable brilliance and beauty; the attention of Christians will be riveted on him. Boston observes how the wise men fell down and worshipped Jesus as a young child but, he explains, 'What a ravishing sight will it be to see Him in His kingdom, on His throne, at the Father's right hand.'[18]

There is more. The glory of God will shine through that glorified body 'and the joys of heaven', to quote Boston again, 'spring out from it, to the saints, who shall see and enjoy God in Christ'. No human words or thought here on earth can describe adequately that glorious sight, but the hymn-writer has got it right when she declares:

> The bride eyes not her garment,
> But her dear bridegroom's face;
> I will not gaze at glory,
> But on my King of grace;
> Not at the crown he giveth,
> But on his pierced hand:
> The Lamb is all the glory
> Of Immanuel's Land.
>
> (Anne Ross Cousin, 1824-1906)

To see the Lord in this way will be heaven indeed. Augustine gives expression to this hope in the following words: 'Christ shall be the end of all our longing and desire. Him shall we perpetually see. Him shall we love without tediousness and grief and Him shall we praise without ending.'[19] That will be heaven.

21.
Heaven: relief and Sabbath-rest

That word 'rest' can have a comforting and welcome significance on all kinds of occasions. One such occasion I remember only too well. It was an extremely hot summer's day and,
with a small group, I was hill-walking. The walk took us longer
than expected and at times it was steep. Twice we rested for a
few minutes; it was really delightful to sit or lie on the grass
and rest, even if only briefly. What was even more enjoyable
was at the end when we could sit and rest. It was bliss and
there was no more climbing or scrambling to do. Our happiness was evident for all to see.

Did you know that an important feature of heaven for Christians will be its rest? For many Christians, the journey to heaven
involves a long, arduous climb and struggle. However, in
heaven itself they will rest, and rest permanently, from their
struggles and labours. In this chapter we are going to explore
what the Bible says about this aspect of heaven as a rest, but
we must begin at the beginning.

A gracious invitation

The most famous Bible statement about rest comes from the
lips of the Lord Jesus Christ in the earlier part of his earthly

ministry. The Lord had been preaching and also performing miracles in the area of Galilee, especially in the towns of Korazin, Bethsaida and Capernaum. Sadly, the people in these towns were not interested in his message. Capernaum, for example, was an important town on the shore of the Sea of Galilee; through this town, the important trade route ran from Damascus to the Mediterranean. People in Capernaum were, therefore, prosperous and satisfied with what they had. After all, what else did they need besides a job, money, a home, family and pleasure? They were not concerned about their need to be right with God. Nor did they realize that Jesus was God's Son and the only one who could save them. Their disinterestedness and lack of response led the Lord Jesus to express a 'dirge' over these towns in Matthew 11:20-24.

Then immediately he prayed to the Father. He was not bitter or resentful about the indifference of the people, but rather thankful that the Father had revealed spiritual truths to 'little children', that is, to 'the less sophisticated and less important'.[1] These had consequently felt their emptiness and helplessness as sinners and had then turned to the Son of God for salvation.

Verse 27 records the profound statement of the Lord Jesus in which he shows that he alone has, and knows, what all sinners need. 'All things have been committed to me by my Father. No one knows the Son except the Father, and no one knows the Father except the Son and those to whom the Son chooses to reveal him.'

This is followed by the 'gracious invitation' in verses 28-30: 'Come to me, all you who are weary and burdened, and I will give you rest. Take my yoke upon you and learn from me, for I am gentle and humble in heart, and you will find rest for your souls. For my yoke is easy and my burden is light.'

You have probably observed that the invitation is addressed to those who are 'weary' and 'burdened'. Fatigue and exhaustion are the ideas underlying the first word while the second word is linked with a ship's cargo-load, or burden, which could be extremely heavy. Together the two words refer to those individuals who are exhausted and weighed down by the burdens of guilt, sin, shame, despair and helplessness with regard to the holy God and their desperate need of salvation. They do not know where to turn. But one thing they know: they cannot save themselves and man-made religions or rules do not help at all. What must such people do to be saved? 'Come to me,' the Lord Jesus underlines. No one else can help. He is the only Saviour of sinners. And it is to him, not to a church or Christians, that sinners must go in trust. To such who respond in faith, Christ says, 'I will give you rest.' This is repeated at the end of the next verse: 'And you will find rest for your souls.' These are wonderful words.

The word 'rest' used by the Lord here is *anapausis*. While it includes the idea of rest, yet it more accurately conveys the meaning of relief and refreshment. It means that guilty consciences can be relieved because the law of God that condemns us has been satisfied by Jesus Christ; sins can be forgiven, the past can be covered with mercy, and hope given to those in despair. And there is nothing difficult to do. You do not have to achieve or win anything before going to Christ. He asks us only to come to him; yes, to come to him as we are and in our guilt and sin. His promise is true: 'I will give you rest' and relief for your souls here and then, finally, in heaven. Have you responded personally to this invitation? Remember that only those who respond in faith to Christ will enter the rest of heaven.

Sabbath-rest

The letter of Hebrews has one great theme, namely, the absolute supremacy of Jesus Christ, God's Son, over angels and humans. Consequently, Christ's covenant, his priesthood and his sacrifice are superior to those under the old administration of Moses, or anyone else. Jesus Christ is supreme and he is the only Saviour. But this teaching about Christ in Hebrews is not intended as theological fodder for detached and academic study. Far from it! The teaching has a very practical purpose: the readers are being warned not to give up the Christian faith and return to their old Jewish religion. Rather, they must persevere in faith and obedience despite all the difficulties and persecution they are experiencing. Hebrews 3:7-18, therefore, is a warning against unbelief and includes a strong exhortation: 'See to it, brothers, that none of you has a sinful, unbelieving heart that turns away from the living God' (v. 12).

For those Jews in the Old Testament narrative, entering the 'rest' meant entering Canaan under Joshua's leadership, defeating their enemies and settling peacefully into their new surroundings. It is clear, however, that the 'rest' spoken of in Psalm 95 and in Hebrews chapters 3 and 4 is not the earthly Canaan. 'For if Joshua had given them rest,' the author argues, 'God would not have spoken later about another day' (Heb. 4:8). There is, then, a powerful contrast here between the temporal, earthly 'rest' which God gave to Israel under Joshua and the more glorious, permanent rest reserved in heaven for Christians.

Interestingly, throughout chapters 3 and 4 the author of Hebrews uses a different but related word for 'rest' from that which the Lord Jesus used in Matthew 11. While the Lord used the word *anapausis*, thus highlighting the idea of relief as well as rest, here the word *katapausis* is used to emphasize the fact of rest and the absence of work or exertion. But in Hebrews 4:9 another word, *sabbatismos*, is introduced in the all-important statement: 'There remains, then, a Sabbath-rest for the people of God.' This translation is a good one, for the word means a Sabbath-rest, or observing the Sabbath. Just as God 'rested' after completing his work of creation so

Christians, when they complete their work and service in this world, will enter into God's rest in heaven.

I want to emphasize and illustrate this aspect of heaven as a 'Sabbath-rest'. When my children were small, my wife and I were eager to show them that we enjoyed the Sabbath day. We really looked forward to it. For us, Sunday was a special day; it was often a very happy day, too. There were important biblical reasons why we attached such importance to the Sabbath. One reason is that God established it as a unique day in the week. And God did this at the very beginning. After completing the work of creation, the Bible informs us that 'God blessed the seventh day and made it holy, because on it he rested from all the work of creating that he had done' (Gen. 2:3). The Sabbath was not, then, a primitive, tribal custom but a divinely ordained and permanent provision. This provision was confirmed by God in one of the Ten Commandments. John Calvin observes in this respect: 'There is no commandment the observance of which the Almighty more strictly enforces… The observance of it He eulogizes in the highest terms, and hence, among other divine privileges the faithful set an extraordinary value on the revelation of the Sabbath.'[2] We were also aware of our Lord's words: 'The Sabbath was made for man…' (Mark 2:27). The implication is that we all need a day of rest, one in seven. In the early church, the Christian Sabbath was changed to a Sunday in order to celebrate the resurrection of the Lord Jesus from the dead on that day (see Matt. 28:1-7; Mark 16:9; Luke 24:1-8; John 20:1-9,19). The principle of the Lord's day is the same but for Christians it assumes even richer significance by observing it on a Sunday.

It was for these and other reasons that my wife and I wanted our children to honour but also enjoy the Sabbath day. To help make the point, a few words in Welsh were put to song and in translation they were:

Hooray! Hooray! Hooray!
Sunday is coming, Sunday is coming,
Hooray! Hooray! Hooray!

They were not profound words but they expressed on a
Saturday our joy and expectation that Sunday, the Lord's day,
was almost upon us, and it was a special day with many privileges. We could spend the day together as a family; there was
no work to do and no school to attend. It was prime time to be
together as a family and enjoy one another. As a family too,
we went to the church services together. We worshipped the
Lord, heard his Word preached and shared fellowship with
many other Christians. The day was set apart to the Lord for
worship and for our own spiritual, physical and emotional benefit. Quite often, friends joined us for a family meal and the
fellowship was enriched. It really was a Sabbath-rest.

I remember vividly sharing this illustration in the Korean
conference referred to in the opening chapter of this book.
My aim was to show them that the Sabbath day pointed to,
and was a foretaste of, heaven. And they understood the point.
As the meeting ended and we walked slowly to the cafeteria
for lunch, many of the ministers were deeply moved and approached me excitedly: 'Hooray', they exclaimed with joy, 'we
are going to heaven. Hooray!'

And we should rejoice in anticipating the Sabbath-rest of
heaven. There will be no exhausting or dreary work to do
there. All God's family will be present and we shall perfectly
enjoy the Lord's fellowship and grace. No matter how precious
and enjoyable our Sabbath days are here in this world, remember that they are only a shadow of that glorious Sabbath-rest
we shall enjoy in heaven. In the next chapter we will examine
in more detail the bliss of heaven's rest by considering the
statement in Revelation 14:13.

22.
Heaven: glorious rest

In continuing the theme of heaven's rest, we are going to reflect in this chapter on the important statement in Revelation 14:13: 'Then I heard a voice from heaven say, "Write: Blessed are the dead who die in the Lord from now on." "Yes," says the Spirit, "they will rest from their labour, for their deeds will follow them." '

The context of this statement

This statement is found in a chapter where the victory of God's church is being emphasized and illustrated. The note of victory here is emphatic and thrilling. First of all, the entire church of Christ is pictured symbolically as consisting of 144,000 (Rev. 14:1-5). This number should not be taken literally, for it represents the complete and vast number of believers in all ages who have been chosen and redeemed in Christ. The church is pictured as being clean, faithful and engaged in heaven in praising the Lord with a 'new song'.

A second picture in verses 6-11 is different for it is one of awful judgement. Three angels are involved; one angel proclaims the 'eternal gospel' (v. 6), while another two angels announce judgement on the unbelieving nations. The punishment is dreadful: unbelievers 'will drink of the wine of God's fury' and will be 'tormented ... for ever and ever' (see vv. 10-11).

The contrast in the passage

Almost unexpectedly, after the punishment of unbelievers is announced, the apostle John hears the comforting words of verse 13. The contrast between punishment for unbelievers, on the one hand, and blessedness and rest for believers, on the other, is a powerful one. And this contrast is continued in verses 14-20, where angels are described as carrying out at the Lord's command his punishment on all unbelieving people.

Notice how the contrast is introduced in verse 13: 'Then I heard a voice from heaven...' This was the voice of God, a reliable voice, the voice of authority and truth. Perhaps you feel confused at present because of the conflicting voices of political, social and religious leaders. Who is right? Where can I find truth? Can reliable answers ever be found to the basic questions of life and death? You may be afraid of being deceived or brainwashed by bizarre cults. It is an understandable reaction, for there are real dangers and you must exercise great caution. For example, in 1978 as many as 913 members of the 'People's Temple' cult obeyed the orders of their leader, the Rev. Jim Jones, to kill themselves by drinking cyanide in the forests of Guyana. It was a foolish and unnecessary thing to do, but the people were victims of deception on the part of their leader. Sadly, such disasters occur at regular intervals. Think of Waco in 1993, the Solar Temple incidents in Switzerland in 1994, or the Aum Shinrikyo religious cult in Japan responsible for the sarin poison nerve-gas attack on the Tokyo subway trains in 1995 which killed ten people and injured nearly six thousand. What the apostle John hears, however, is not a religious guru, a clever philosopher or an eloquent politician, but God himself speaking. And we can hear God speaking today, but only in the Bible. That is where God has spoken reliably and revealed his character and purpose. Here is light which shines in the darkness of this world to give us certain, truthful answers to ultimate questions about life and death.

And what John hears from God is concerning 'the dead'. Without doubt, this is a crucial subject. Death faces everyone; there is no escape from it. Death is an enemy and frightens many people; it casts its shadow over our lives and snatches our relatives and friends from us. We need to hear a reliable word from God that explains death, prepares us for it and offers hope. However, what John hears about is the death of a specific people, namely those 'who die in the Lord'. Here are people who have a special relationship to the Lord Jesus Christ and they are described as being 'in the Lord'. This is an important technical term in the New Testament describing the fact that Christians trust Christ and enjoy a personal, intimate and spiritual union with the Lord Jesus Christ. There is a history to this relationship as well. When God the Father chose a people to be saved, he did so 'in him', that is, in Christ, 'before the creation of the world' (Eph. 1:4). But there is more to it. God's elect were in Christ, too, when he died for them and rose again from the dead (see Rom. 6:2-11; Eph. 2:4-6; Col. 3:3-4). This is applied and made real to each person chosen by the Father in Christ. And this occurs when God calls and brings us effectively to Christ by new birth and conversion. Such people, in dependence upon Christ, are able to obey and please the Lord; then, at the end, they die 'in the Lord', that is, in fellowship with him.

It is not, however, the dying which is emphasized for John in the words of Revelation 14:13 but rather what death brings. An illustration may help to make the point clear. When on occasions I work a long way from home for a few days or

weeks at a time, I always look forward to the return journey.
Now that is not because I enjoy travel. In fact, whether it is an
aeroplane, train or coach I use, the means of transport is important to me only for the reason that it will take me home.
My heart is with my family and I long to be with them. Similarly, for the Christian it is not the actual dying which is important, but the fact that through death he goes home to heaven.

The comfort in this statement

Two reasons are given to us in Revelation 14:13 as to why it is
'blessed' for Christians to die and I want you to feel their
comfort and reassurance.

1. They will rest from their labour

That in itself should be a great comfort, for Christians will rest
from their labours in heaven in a number of ways.

For example, *we shall not need to struggle against sin in
our own lives* when we reach heaven. Before we became Christians, sin controlled us and separated us from God; each part
of our lives was affected and polluted by it. A transformation
then took place when we were born again of the Holy Spirit;
that was a radical, inward, supernatural work which broke
sin's power and gave us a new nature with grace to love and
obey the Lord. Of course, we did not become perfect, but our
lives were different.

It was not long, however, before we realized that sin was
still active within us, dragging us down, tempting and drawing
us away from prayer and obedience, encouraging us to speak,
behave and think in ways we were ashamed of. A battle continues to rage within us and it is especially fierce on occasions.
We struggle to deny self, to put away sins from our lives, but

it is still hard and we often fail. Just like the apostle Paul, we can exclaim with anguish, 'For what I want to do I do not do, but what I hate I do... When I want to do good, evil is right there with me' (Rom. 7:15,21). But it will not always be like that, for when we die we shall then, in heaven, be free from all personal sin and have no need to struggle against sin. We shall rest from such labour.

Furthermore, in heaven *we shall as Christians have no need to fight and oppose the devil*, our great enemy. In this world we have to 'take [our] stand against the devil's schemes. For our struggle is not against flesh and blood, but against the rulers, against the authorities, against the powers of this dark world and against the spiritual forces of evil in the heavenly realms' (Eph. 6:11-12). The devil is a 'liar and the father of lies' and 'a murderer from the beginning' and 'there is no truth in him' (John 8:44). He is our enemy and he works hard to tempt us and to spoil the Lord's work. 'The devil knows where I live,' was the honest testimony of the Cornish evangelist Billy Bray. Christians must therefore 'be alert', and 'resist' the devil continually (1 Peter 5:8-9; James 4:7) until the moment they die. But in heaven Christians will be beyond the reach and influence of the devil, so we shall have relief from the labour of resisting the devil.

There is another way in which we shall rest in heaven: *we shall not have to fight against worldliness*. 'Do not love the world or anything in the world' (1 John 2:15) is a clear directive to God's people. Here the term 'world' represents all that is opposed and contrary to God's holy nature and purpose. And it is not merely doing something obviously worldly, like gambling, or stealing, or reading 'porn'. It also includes thoughts and desires which are contrary to the principles of the Bible. For example, do we manage our businesses in ways that please God? Are our families and homes run in loving, Christ-honouring ways? How do we spend our money? Are we indulgent and selfish, or do we use our money wisely as God's stewards and give sacrificially to the Lord's work? What about our time? Do we waste this, too? Christians have to struggle to honour God rather than themselves in these areas of worldliness. It is a fight. Effort, sacrifice, discipline, prayer and perseverance are necessary because the world opposes the church and individual Christians. The world also comes into the church and into our hearts in so many subtle as well as obvious ways. Christians should resist and fight against the world. Only death will bring an end to this struggle and then in heaven we shall be in a place where only holiness, love and God-centred activities exist. That will be rest for us.

The rest in heaven will apply to us in another way as well. *There will be no disappointments or difficult circumstances* for us to cope with in heaven; *nor will there be sickness, sadness or death* there. Here in this life Christians struggle to trust God and to submit to providences which are often unwelcome and painful. An unsuccessful interview, redundancy, ill-health, a broken relationship, friends who let us down, inadequate income, the death of a loved one are all experiences in which Christians continually struggle to trust and honour God. Our hearts can break at times because of the pressures. Rebellion arises in our hearts against God and we have to fight through to believe that 'In all things God works for the good of those who love him' (Rom. 8:28). But it is not easy. And there is much we do not at present understand about the ways of God. It is often a struggle. But listen to the marvellous news: we shall rest in heaven from such labours and difficulties. The conditions there will be perfect. Nothing will ever disappoint us or cause us problems in heaven; even Christians, who are often inconsistent and disappointing here, will be free from all sin and oddities. There will be no need for us to struggle any more with problems relating to providence and people; that will be rest!

A final illustration of rest can be given. Here in this world Christians have to take seriously the Lord's command to 'Go into all the world and preach the good news to all...' (Mark 16:15; Matt. 28:19-20). It is an urgent task. Each year over thirty million people throughout the world die. Each time the second hand of my watch moves, a person dies and goes either to heaven or hell. Some Christians take this task of evangelism seriously. They pray hard for people to be saved; they invite their friends, neighbours and relatives to hear the gospel preached. Quite naturally, in conversation, these Christians will sometimes speak of Christ and his unique death for sinners. With their churches Christians are also involved in ongoing evangelistic work in youth groups or house-visitation or open-air preaching. Their energies are thrown into the work of winning people to Christ. And some are called by God to full-time evangelism in cross-cultural situations, often a long way from home. There is sacrifice, effort, zeal, commitment, compassion, as well as emotional, and sometimes physical, strains in taking the gospel to people. But such labours will end when we die. In heaven *we shall no longer need compassion for unbelievers, nor shall we engage in evangelism* from heaven. We shall rest from our labours.

2. Their deeds will follow them

The second reason for comfort in Revelation 14:13 is that 'Their deeds will follow them.' In other words, the good work which Christians have done in this world will continue to be useful and effective even after they go to heaven. This is true in many ways, but here are two examples to encourage you.

Charles Spurgeon was a faithful Christian and a powerful Baptist preacher. He was used greatly to help many thousands of people through his preaching. But his deeds still follow in the sense that his printed sermons and the challenge of his life continue to influence many people in profound ways.

There are many other examples relating to ordinary Christians. Take the case of a godly young wife who gave birth to five children. Her longing was that each child should become a Christian and serve the Lord. Despite the demands of the home, she prayed much for her children; she also taught them the Word daily and was a great example to those young lives. They were taken to church and shown how to value the means of grace. At the age of sixty-seven the mother died and went to her 'rest' with the Lord. However, that is not the end of the story, for her works 'follow' her. Her prayers were answered. The children themselves became committed Christians. And they still talk about their mother, especially her example and strong faith. They deliberately try to practise in their lives what their mother taught them. In so many ways, the 'works' of their mother 'follow' her and continue to help and challenge the children.

Nothing we do for Christ will be wasted. Our prayers, our acts of obedience, our Sunday school lessons, our sermons, our gifts, our faltering words in pointing people to the gospel and our times of family worship will all bear fruit to his glory, even after we die. Such fruit may be unseen and unknown to us now, but one thing is certain: 'Your labour in the Lord is not in vain' (1 Cor. 15:58). Be comforted by these precious truths!

23.
Heaven: our work there

As we saw in the previous chapter, heaven is a rest, but it is a rest from conflict, struggling, fighting, repenting and self-denying. With such factors entirely removed from us in heaven, it is going to be unbounded pleasure, as well as a rest, for Christians to serve and worship the Lord there. In this chapter I want to focus on three important areas of Christian activity in heaven — namely, worship, service and fellowship.

1. Worship

I can only imagine what it will be like to worship in heaven with so many Christians. About six years ago I preached in one church in Eastern Europe which was crowded with Christians. They thoroughly enjoyed singing the praises of the Lord Jesus. Joy was written all over their faces. And the people obviously meant every word they were singing. Under the preaching of the Word also these Christians were attentive and responsive. It was genuine worship.

Or I think of some precious minutes in a ministers' conference. The Word preached was powerful and we were all made deeply aware of Christ's love and sacrifice for his church. When the preacher finished speaking, we sang a closing hymn of praise. We repeated the hymn a second time, then a third time. No one seemed to want to stop singing that hymn. Then, after prayer, we all sat down and there followed a deafening silence. Nobody moved and not one person wanted to speak. A sense of awe, astonishment and appreciation filled our hearts. It was certainly a time of real and unforgettable worship. Only reluctantly did we eventually leave the room to have a meal.

These examples are only a foretaste of heaven where we shall be engaged in rapturous worship. The book of Revelation gives us a helpful insight into the subject as it contains as many as fourteen songs and expressions of worship in heaven. In chapter 4:7-11 we are given the first glimpse of heavenly worship. The 'four living creatures' mentioned in verse 6 are probably high-ranking angels, whereas the twenty-four elders represent the entire church of Jesus Christ. Both the angels and the church triumphant in heaven are united in their undivided, fervent worship of God. They worship with deep reverence and 'fall down before' the holy, sovereign, eternal Creator God.

Revelation 5 records three songs which are sung in turn by the angels and the church in unison (vv. 8-10), the angels alone (vv. 11-12) and all creation (v. 13), with the climactic shout of 'Amen' from the angels followed by worship and prostration on the part of the church. The worship is Christ-centred: 'You are worthy... Worthy is the Lamb, who was slain...' (vv. 9,12). Our redemption was purchased for us by Christ; we owe all to him and therefore in heaven we shall want to engage in endless worship of our Mediator.

Notice that it is a 'new song' which the church sings in heaven. It is new 'because never before had such a great and glorious deliverance been accomplished and never before had the Lamb received this great honour'.[1] It is new also because it is a new phase in the application of redemption. Here the church is complete, the end of the world has arrived, the last battles for the Lord have been fought and all the elect are safe in heaven. Death is conquered, the enemies of the Lord are finally subdued and punished, while Christ is seen and declared by all to be the conqueror. It will be a joy to worship such a God. And there we shall praise and love him as we ought. We shall no longer be hindered by tired bodies, wandering thoughts, indwelling sin, pressing duties, or the enticements of the world.

John Newton captures both the honest realism of our worship in this world and the perfection of heavenly worship:

Weak is the effort of my heart,
And cold my warmest thought;
But when I see thee as thou art,
I'll praise thee as I ought.

And it is true; heaven's worship will be thrilling and perfect.

2. Service

There are two significant statements on this aspect of the subject in the book of Revelation. The first is in chapter 7:15, where we are informed that Christians in heaven 'are before the throne of God and serve him day and night in his temple'. The statement is pregnant with meaning. One thing to notice is that we shall be close to the Lord, for that is the force of the preposition '*before* the throne of God'. Sometimes when I attend university ceremonies where a famous dignitary is present, I sit in the background with little prospect of meeting the person or getting close to him. On a few other occasions, however, it is different because I am introduced to the famous person and can spend a little time talking with him, even sitting near him on the platform. In heaven we shall be close to the Lord and, in the closest fellowship, we shall have the privilege of serving him continually. There will be no distance between us. The 'temple' referred to is not a building but heaven and the entire new creation where the Lord dwells. While no details are given here as to the ways in which we 'serve' the Lord in heaven, we have already seen that worship will be an essential part of our service.

A similar statement about serving is found in Revelation 22:3: 'And his servants will serve him.' The usual Greek word for servants in the New Testament is *doulos* and it is used often by the apostle Paul to describe the relationship of Christians to the Lord Jesus (see, e.g., Eph. 6:6; Phil. 1:1; Col. 4:12).[2] While *doulos* is used in Revelation 22:3 and is rightly translated as 'servants', yet it is not the verbal form of *doulos* which is used for 'serve' but rather the verb *latreuo*. The same expression is used in chapter 7:15, a verse to which we have already drawn attention. The verb *latreuo* includes the idea of service, like *doulos*, but in the New Testament it exclusively emphasizes divine service and worship (e.g. Matt. 4:10; Luke 2:37; Acts 24:14; 26:7; 27:23; and especially Heb. 9:14; 12:28; 13:10).

No detailed picture is given concerning the ways in which we shall serve the Lord in heaven and we must not indulge in speculation. However, the general picture is clear. We shall always be in the Lord's presence and 'serve him day and night'. Worship will form the major part of this service. There are also hints of responsibilities being given to Christians in heaven such as judging and ruling (Matt. 19:28; 25:21) as well as using God-given talents (Matt. 13:12). It is a glorious prospect: worship, service and fellowship in a perfect place and in the presence of a glorious God. And we shall be without personal sin or fatigue.

The Rev. Kenneth Macrae was the Free Church of Scotland minister in Stornoway in the Isle of Lewis, Scotland, from 1931 to 1964. His long ministry in what was one of the largest

Presbyterian congregations in the world was powerful and fruitful. About five months before his death in early May 1964, he
dictated the following words of testimony: '... I have been
long in His service here, but I never tired of it. All my grief
was that it was so poor, so listless, so forgetful, and so lacking
in holiness; but soon I shall serve Him with a perfect service
without failure or flaw.'[3] That will be heaven indeed!

3. Fellowship

The word 'fellowship' translates the rich Greek word *koinonia*
and includes two important strands of thought.

One strand is that of 'participation' and highlights the idea
that people share in a common experience or possession. For
example, in Jude 3 the word is used and interestingly translated as 'common' by the Authorized Version and the New
King James Version translators: 'our common salvation'. Both
here and in heaven all Christians will participate in this one
glorious salvation provided by the Lord.

A second strand focuses on the idea of sharing, namely,
that we share with others this divine salvation. While salvation
is applied to us personally by the Lord and is appropriated
individually by us through faith, yet we also share this salvation with other Christians. It is in this sense that the apostle
Paul explains in 1 Corinthians 9:23: 'I do all this for the sake
of the gospel, that I may *share* in its blessings' (italics mine).
He is a fellow-sharer with the Corinthian Christians in the gospel. In this way the corporate aspect is emphasized but it is
going to be realized perfectly in heaven.

Ponder this fact briefly: heaven is going to be populated by
'a great multitude that no one could count, from every nation,
tribe, people and language' (Rev. 7:9). Earlier they are described as being 144,000 in number (v. 4: see also 14:1) but

this number is symbolic and represents completeness, that is, Christians throughout history who have believed in Jesus Christ. Only God knows the precise number of his elect, but it is a number which is so vast that no human is able to count them. This is thrilling, for sometimes in this world we may be the only Christian family in an area, or the only Christian in work, and even the church to which we belong may be small and discouraging. But we shall not be lonely or isolated in heaven, for there will be 'a great multitude' of Christians from all nations there. And by the end of world history the church will be complete in heaven. It will be exciting to see so many Christians.

Nor will there be limits on the time we spend together in fellowship there. For purposes of sleep, food, work or family commitments, our informal and formal times of fellowship have to be restricted and sometimes we are compelled to separate from Christians for a considerable period of time, especially if they live a long way from us. That was the experience of the leaders of the Ephesus church when the apostle Paul bade them farewell at Miletus. They wept and longed for their beloved leader to continue with them in fellowship and ministry, but it was not possible (see Acts 20:17-38). In heaven, however, our fellowship will continue uninterrupted with no more partings or restrictions.

And it will be perfect fellowship too. There will be no quarrels or divisions amongst Christians, nor will we want to criticize or exclude other Christians. No Christian will feel neglected or offended. Nothing will divide us there, and certainly not denominations, or baptism, or charismata; there will be perfect agreement and intimate fellowship.

24.
Heaven: we live there!

Our family discussions on the matter of a summer family holiday can be extensive but interesting. Some potential holiday destinations are regarded as boring by the children; other places are at least possibilities, so we discuss the pros and cons of going to various locations. The final decision is usually determined by factors such as cost, availability, distance and, of course, whether there will be interesting things for us to do there or not.

Well, what about heaven in this respect? What will we do there? After all, Christians are going to be there for a very long time, so what, if anything, will we be doing in heaven? Will it be boring? These questions arise quite naturally in our minds and they are also useful in stimulating us to think more deeply about heaven. Such questions are beneficial in another way too, for they make us go back to the Bible for our answers.

An obvious question

Before we attempt an answer, there is an obvious question which must be answered: if heaven consists of rest for Christians, how can they at the same time also be active and serve the Lord there? It is a good question and we can answer it immediately.

Relief and rest will be important features of heaven, but this does not mean that Christians will be idle or lazy there. And they will certainly not be bored. With the burden, hardships and conflict involved in our earthly pilgrimage completely removed, to serve and worship the Lord in heaven will be sheer delight as well as a rest. In other words, heaven is not a complete rest from labour, but a rest from conflict, struggling, fighting and repenting.

We shall live

What then shall we do in heaven? In the previous chapter we saw that in heaven all Christians will be active in worship, service and fellowship. In this chapter, I intend to draw attention to one rather obvious point, but it is a point that needs to be emphasized: we shall *live* in heaven. Heaven means life — eternal life, and resurrection life! Christians will live life to the full in heaven and for ever.

In Bunyan's classic *Pilgrim's Progress*, Christian was eager to avoid hell and to free himself of his burden of sin, so he set out to search for salvation and eternal life. After receiving helpful directions from Evangelist, Christian was begged by his relatives to return home. His burden, however, was too heavy for him to return home; instead, he carried on and shouted, 'Life! Life! Eternal Life!' He soon reached the cross, and obtained forgiveness as well as eternal life. But this life is a gift: 'The gift of God is eternal life in Christ Jesus our Lord' (Rom. 6:23). It begins with the divine, heavenly life brought to us by the Holy Spirit in the new birth; it is a life that never dies but is perfected in heaven. In one of his printed sermons,

Spurgeon speaks of the great difference between the Christian
who has just received eternal life and the mature Christian,
but he adds, 'It is the same life.'¹ Spurgeon continues, 'The
life of believers in heaven, the life that never sins, the life that
is absolute obedience, the life that is undiluted bliss, is exactly
the same life that is in the believer now.'

Life! Heaven teems with life. The living God is there, as is
the risen Christ who conquered death and hell. Christians live
life to the full in such a glorious place. Nothing ever dies there.
And eventually all Christians will have their bodies raised and
transformed to the likeness of Christ's glorious body (Phil.
3:21). With bodies and souls reunited, Christians will enjoy
life there that is infinitely rich, satisfying and also unending.

Preaching in early October 1885 immediately following the
death of the Earl of Shaftesbury, Spurgeon began by drawing
attention to the earl's personal piety, his love of people and his
deep concern for the oppressed. Spurgeon's text was then taken
from the words of the Lord Jesus in Luke 20:37-38: 'But in
the account of the bush, even Moses showed that the dead
rise, for he calls the Lord "the God of Abraham, and the God
of Isaac, and the God of Jacob". He is not the God of the
dead, but of the living, for to him all are alive.' The preacher
unfolded these profound words in three ways. First of all, he
showed that a glorious relationship is declared here between
God and these three patriarchs. Secondly, he emphasized how
eternal life was implied in the statement: 'He is not the God of
the dead but of the living.' The preacher added, 'A living God
is the God of living men; and Abraham, Isaac and Jacob are
still alive.'² Thirdly, Spurgeon explains how the text unveils,
even if only 'scantily', 'the glorious life' of heaven. For
example, Abraham, Isaac and Jacob live *personally*, as individuals in heaven, not as part of one great mass of people.
'God is the God of saints, as living distinct lives,' adds
Spurgeon. 'Abraham is Abraham, Isaac is Isaac, Jacob is

Jacob.'[3] Furthermore, these patriarchs are *mentioned by their names*, so they are distinct and recognizable in heaven. And that will be true of all Christians there. We shall recognize and know each other in glory. Even though Moses and Elijah had gone to glory hundreds of years earlier, they had not lost their personalities or their names but were recognized by the disciples on the Mount of Transfiguration (Matt. 17:3-4). Christians who die, therefore, are very much alive in heaven and do not lose their individuality. As you mourn and miss Christian relatives and weep at their gravesides, remember that only their bodies remain. They themselves are alive in heaven and to be with Christ 'is better by far' (Phil. 1:23).

25.
Heaven: a better country

Heaven is a place; it is also a country. That is one way in which heaven is described in Hebrews 11:14-16. Once again the immediate context is significant and it is important to appreciate why heaven is described in terms of a country in this section.

The context

The whole of Hebrews 11 can be called a chapter of faith for we are introduced to many different men and women of faith in the Old Testament period. In the most remarkable and challenging circumstances, these believers trusted in God implicitly and relied wholly on his promises. From verses 8-19 in the chapter the focus is on Abraham. God's call to Abraham to leave the security of his home area was a demanding one; he had to uproot himself and his family and go to an unspecified location hundreds of miles away. Astonishingly, there was no hesitation on Abraham's part. We are informed that he 'obeyed and went, even though he did not know where he was going' (v. 8).

There were obvious encouragements for this man of faith. For one thing, he knew that God would help and direct him; he would not be on his own, nor would he be let down by his

God. A second encouragement related to a promise divinely given to him. This promise assured Abraham that the territory he eventually reached 'he would later receive as his inheritance'.

There was, however, a snag. This promise was not given until after Abraham had left his home area in Ur of the Chaldeans. In fact, the promise was not given until months later when he reached Shechem in the promised land of Canaan (see Gen. 12:6-7). Later, after his return from Egypt, the promise was repeated to Abraham and amplified in an exciting way. 'Lift up your eyes from where you are and look north and south, east and west,' the Lord told him. 'All the land that you see I will give to you and your offspring for ever.' There followed immediately a command to Abraham before the promise was again underlined: 'Go, walk through the length and breadth of the land, for I am giving it to you' (Gen. 13:14-17). Some time later the promise was repeated but accompanied by the added promise that he would one day have a son and heir (Gen. 15:2-6,18-21). Years later, some months prior to the birth of his son Isaac, the promise of the country was repeated in a divine covenant established with Abraham: 'The whole land of Canaan, where you are now an alien, I will give ... to you and your descendants...' (Gen. 17:8).

In Hebrews 11:9 the story is resumed. After his long initial journey, Abraham obediently 'made his home in the promised land' but — and it is important to recognize the fact — 'like a stranger in a foreign country'. The country of Canaan belonged to Abraham now only in the form of promise; he did not receive the actual possession of the country. Nevertheless, this man of faith lived in the light of the promise, yet as a resident alien, 'like a stranger in a foreign country'. I can appreciate the point in a small way. When I landed at a busy Asian airport for the first time, my progress was slow in moving through customs and immigration. There were no problems but I felt that I did not belong to the country. It all seemed so strange

— the language, the people and even some of the formalities. Then my eyes focused on large signs above the immigration corridors where I was waiting to show my passport. Two signs especially spoke to me in that situation: one sign was simply 'Foreigners' and the other sign was 'Nationals'. And I was a foreigner visiting the country for a brief period. That was how Abraham felt, 'a stranger in a foreign country'.

What was the secret for Abraham? Not only was it the fact of his faith, but also his persistence in trusting God and continually, patiently relying on his promise. Here is the emphasis of Hebrews 11:10, where it is clear that Abraham's faith was settled on a heavenly rather than a temporal country or city. He looked for a city of a different kind, one with enduring foundations, 'whose architect and builder is God'. For Abraham, the earthly Canaan and its promise pointed to a more glorious and eternal inheritance promised in the future. In verse 13 we are informed that all these believers, including Abraham, 'were still living by faith when they died'. Their lives were ruled by the conviction that God would honour his promise; even in dying they continually looked forward to this fulfilment. For this reason they lived in this world primarily as 'aliens and strangers'. Their quest, according to verse 14, was a 'country' and homeland, but not Canaan or their original home. 'Instead, they were longing for a better country — a heavenly one,' and their hearts were set on it.

The apostle Paul gives us a New Testament perspective on the subject. Drawing a contrast between Christians and those who are 'enemies of the cross of Christ', the apostle observes that for the latter 'Their mind is on earthly things' (Phil. 3:19). That is their world — the world of the here and now which is sensual and shameful, material and temporary. 'Their destiny is destruction,' is the stark announcement concerning their future.

By contrast, for Christians, 'Our citizenship is in heaven' (Phil. 3:20). It is true that we have a nationality in at least one

country in this world and that we are citizens within a certain
city or community. There are responsibilities we have to fulfil
within our country and community while at the same time we
enjoy the security and protection of that country. However, in
a far more wonderful way our homeland as Christians is in
heaven.

The names of all Christians are registered in heaven; it is
God in heaven who is responsible for the miraculous new birth
in the lives of Christians. From heaven, Christians are ruled
and they seek to behave consistently with the standards of
heaven. The protection and well-being of Christians are secured by heaven while the prayers of Christians ascend regularly to heaven.

Many Christians long for heaven while some have already
entered that homeland. 'And we eagerly await a Saviour from
there,' the apostle adds, 'the Lord Jesus Christ who ... will
transform our lowly bodies so that they will be like his glorious body' (Phil. 3:21). Similarly, according to Hebrews 11:16,
Old Testament believers 'were longing for a better country —
a heavenly one'.

Notice here that heaven is described as a '*better* country'.
The word 'better' is a key word in the epistle to the Hebrews
and is often used to express the superiority of the Lord Jesus
over angels (Heb. 1:4) or the superiority of his death over that
of animal sacrifices (12:24). In which ways can we describe
heaven as being a 'better country' than any earthly country? I
suggest that there are at least three ways in which heaven is
better.

The company is better

For one thing, the company is better in terms of the *number*
who will be there. Heaven will not be thinly populated, nor
will it be a small congregation that worships and serves the

Lord there. The apostle John's glimpse of heaven revealed 'a great multitude that no one could count' (Rev. 7:9). It will be a thrill to be with so many Christians.

The company is also better in heaven because it will be thoroughly *international*, 'from every nation, tribe, people and language'. Christians will be there from the West, but many more will come from mainland China, Asia, Eastern Europe, Africa, Australasia and South America.

Heaven's company is also better because of its *completeness*. The whole church of Christ from all ages will one day be safely gathered into heaven and not one Christian will be missing. This means that the famous and the unknown will be there. To meet Moses or Elijah, Paul and Peter, or the thief converted to Christ on the cross, will be humbling. Perhaps then to see John Calvin, Martin Luther, George Whitefield, John Wesley, Charles Spurgeon and Martyn Lloyd-Jones may excite us to praise the God of grace even more. Our Christian relatives and friends will also be there, so the company will be better than anything we have known on earth.

While angels will be present yet, supremely, the company is better in heaven because *the Lord* himself is present. No longer will there be any need for conferences, Christian books, a Bible or preachers, for Christians will see and be with the Lord, 'which is better by far' (Phil. 1:23). The company is better in heaven. Do you not long to go there?

The fellowship is better

Sharing about the Lord with other Christians, praying and reading or hearing the Word together can be immensely enjoyable and exhilarating. True, it is not always so, possibly due to our backsliding, arrogance, doubts, or ungracious words and actions. There are times, however, when being with Christians in church or in informal sharing can be uplifting, even exciting. The memories of such times may still linger with you. Or do you long for some of your Christian friends with whom you can share deeply about the Lord?

Well, whatever your experience of Christian fellowship may have been like, remember that the fellowship of heaven is going to be infinitely better. For one thing, there will be no sin to spoil relationships between Christians; no one will feel offended or give offence to anyone. There will be no disagreements or divisions, no sharp words and certainly no unloving attitudes. Christians in heaven will get on well with each other in perfect love and harmony. Nor will there be any need to part from one another in heaven in order to attend to daily duties. In heaven Christian fellowship will be uninterrupted. And to make it even more wonderful, the Lord will be there in the midst of Christians and he will be seen, admired and worshipped by all. That will be real and glorious fellowship, better than any fellowship previously enjoyed on earth.

The conditions are better

This is an obvious but important point to make. Disease and death, pain, sadness and mourning will have no place in heaven. And at the Lord's return Christians will receive glorified bodies immune from decay and death. In fact, 'He will wipe every tear from their eyes. There will be no more death or mourning or crying or pain, for the old order of things has passed away' (Rev. 21:4). That is heaven, a better country, and Christians can look forward to going there. This is beautifully illustrated in the death of Dr Martyn Lloyd-Jones.

Born in 1899, Lloyd-Jones trained for the medical profession and had an illustrious, though brief, medical career in London before being called to the Christian ministry in Port Talbot in the 1930s and then to Westminster Chapel, London, from 1939 to 1968. His preaching ministry was powerful and influential. Following his retirement in 1968, Dr Lloyd-Jones exercised an itinerant preaching ministry and helped to edit his sermons and addresses for publication.

He died in March 1981 but he approached death with a strong faith and expectancy. Approximately a year before his death, he explained to his biographer, 'We do not give enough time to death and to our going on. It is a very strange thing this: the *one* certainty, yet we do not think about it.'[1] Referring to George Whitefield, he said, 'Whitefield ... had such a knowledge of the coming glory that he desired to be there. That should be true of us all.'[2]

As he became weaker, he was informed on a hospital visit in October 1980 that his remaining time in this world would be brief. In late February 1981 there was a marked deterioration in his physical condition and he refused any further antibiotics, but on one occasion, for example, he pointed to the words of 2 Corinthians 4:16-18: 'For which cause we faint not; but though our outward man perish, yet the inward man is renewed day by day. For our light affliction, which is but for a moment, worketh for us a far more exceeding and eternal weight of glory...' (AV). When asked if that was his experience at the time, he vigorously nodded his head in reply. A day or so later, Lloyd-Jones, with a shaky hand, scribbled some words on a scrap of paper for his family: 'Do not pray for healing. Do not hold me back from the glory.'[3] Within three days he died and entered heaven, that 'better country'.

26.
Heaven: the new Jerusalem

The point was made in the last chapter that heaven is a country, and a better country than any we may live in here on earth. In addition to the three reasons noted in that chapter, there is one further reason why heaven is an infinitely better country: in the future it will be associated with the 'Holy City', or the 'new Jerusalem'. To appreciate this link, it is necessary to look briefly at Revelation chapters 21 and 22, which provide us with 'the most extensive revelation of the eternal home to be found anywhere in the Scriptures'.[1] The context is strongly eschatological, referring to a period immediately following the general judgement (Rev. 20:11). Here is 'the culmination of redemption'.[2]

A word of warning, however, is appropriate at this point. The 'Holy City' is not heaven as such, for it is seen 'coming down out of heaven from God' (Rev. 21:2). Heaven is certainly the origin of this city. No human or earthly organization has designed or established it. Certainly not, for the architect and builder of this future city is God himself (Heb. 11:10).

The Old Testament background

There is an important Old Testament background to this concept of the 'Holy City' or 'new Jerusalem' which we need to

mention briefly. This 'Holy City' is not referred to at all in
Genesis although in Hebrews 11:10 we are informed that
Abraham 'was looking forward to the city with foundations'
(verse 16 identifies this with a 'country' described as a 'heavenly one'). From Judges 1:8,21, it seems that the tribe of Judah
captured the city of Jerusalem; then later David won the nearby
fortress occupied by Jebusites (2 Sam. 5:6-9). It was under
David that Jerusalem was made the Jewish chief city. Vast
improvements were made to the city during David's kingship;
a new palace was built and the ark of the covenant was brought
to the city, symbolizing the Lord's presence. At this time, the
name 'Zion' began to be used, initially with regard to the fortress but later 'becoming a synonym for the whole city'.[3]

The Jews valued the city highly, at times superstitiously,
especially after Solomon built a new and splendid temple there
for divine worship. The history of Jerusalem and its temple
was turbulent, involving capture and partial devastation in 587
B.C. under Nebuchadnezzar, in 167 B.C. under Antiochus IV
and, finally, in A.D. 70, under the Romans. What happened to
this city affected the Jews profoundly; their hopes and joys
were inextricably bound up with it.

> If I forget you, O Jerusalem [declares the psalmist],
>   may my right hand forget its skill.
> May my tongue cling to the roof of my mouth
>   if I do not remember you,
> if I do not consider Jerusalem
>   my highest joy
>
>   (Ps. 137:5-6).

And that was not sentimental jargon intended to impress others;
rather the words expressed the deep regard and love of the
Jewish exiles in Babylon for their beloved city and all its sacred
associations.[4]

The New Testament perspective

The New Testament perspective concerning Jerusalem is somewhat different, in fact more condemnatory, with its destruction in A.D. 70 foretold by the Lord Jesus in Matthew 23:37-39 and 24:1-29. There are still, however, traces of the Old Testament respect for the ancient city. For example, for the Lord's second temptation, 'The devil took him to the holy city' (Matt. 4:5). Some weeks later the Lord himself commanded Christians not to take oaths in the name of heaven or earth 'or by Jerusalem, for it is the city of the Great King' (Matt. 5:35).

A major New Testament reference to the city is found in Hebrews 12:22: 'But you have come to Mount Zion, to the heavenly Jerusalem, the city of the living God...' In the context of warning these professing Hebrew Christians against rejecting the Lord, the writer of the epistle draws a powerful contrast in chapter 12:18-24 between the earthly Sinai and the heavenly Zion. The sight of Sinai on that unique historical occasion terrified the Jews (Exod. 19:16-19; 20:18-21; Deut. 4:11-12) and even filled Moses with awe (Heb. 12:18-21). By contrast, Christians have come by conversion, not to a physical mountain, but to the spiritual and heavenly realm of God. Here and now Christians have eternal life in Jesus Christ who is 'the mediator of a new covenant' (v. 24).

The three terms used in verse 22 are significant. 'Mount Zion' referred originally to the Jebusite fortress which David captured and which became his royal palace as well as the location of the temple. Here was God's dwelling-place. The 'heavenly Jerusalem' emphasizes its spiritual and heavenly nature, to which Christians have access, although its full potential and manifestation will appear when the 'new Jerusalem' appears from heaven. The phrase, 'city of the living God', highlights the dynamic presence and activity of the living God

among his people; life and resurrection are essential features
of this dimension.

The New Jerusalem

It is in Revelation chapter 21 that we find a detailed reference
to 'the Holy City, the new Jerusalem' (v. 2). What is this new
Jerusalem like? Notice that it is described as being 'holy' because no sin or imperfection will be present there; it is also
called a 'city' because it is heavily populated but secure and
well-ruled. It is also the 'new' Jerusalem, for it is not a re-
building of the ancient city but rather the ultimate, glorified
city characterized by the resurrection of believers as well as
the renewal of the heavens and earth.

This 'new Jerusalem' is described as 'coming down out of
heaven from God', so it has unsurpassing beauty just like 'a
bride beautifully dressed for her husband'. Here is a reminder
that the church as a bride will, by this end time, have been
washed clean from all sin and attired in the perfect righteousness of her Bridegroom and Saviour, the Lord Jesus Christ.

Even more glorious will be the fulfilment of God's covenant promise that 'God himself will be with them ...' and
that 'He will live with them' (v. 3). Christians will enjoy the
immediate presence of their God and enjoy uninterrupted, satisfying fellowship with God, while tears, death, mourning and
pain will have been removed for ever (v. 4).

'I am making everything new!' are the words which the
apostle John hears from the throne of heaven (v. 5), emphasizing the fact that it is the sovereign and omnipotent Lord who
will renew the entire creation, establishing perfect, eternal
conditions for the church to enjoy perpetually.

As if to emphasize the certainty of this glorious purpose
being accomplished, the Lord speaks again to John: 'It is done.

I am the Alpha and the Omega, the Beginning and the End'
(v. 6). All that God promises, he achieves; all that he begins,
he completes. Although this promise of glory relates to the
future, it is nevertheless certain and will be accomplished.

The remaining parts of chapters 21 and 22:1-5 mostly describe this future glorious state of the church following the
Lord's return. This future hope, the new Jerusalem, is described
by way of analogy and with rich, often Old Testament, sym-
bolism. It is a breathtaking scene and the glory awaiting the
church is unimaginably beautiful. The church will enjoy an even
more intimate love-relationship with the Lord (21:9). Nor will
a temple be necessary, for the Lord's presence will fill the entire city: 'The glory of God gives it light, and the Lamb is the
lamp' (vv. 22-23).

Yes, heaven is an infinitely better country. And when all of
God's purposes will be finally accomplished at the Lord's return, we shall see 'the new Jerusalem, coming down out of
heaven from God'. Life; resurrection; the abolition of death,
disease, tears and pain; a new earth where only righteousness
exists; happiness; light; the Lord's immediate presence — these
will be the integral features of the new Jerusalem. With glorified bodies, a new heaven and a new earth, a completed and
glorified church, absolute and undisputed victory and rule, the
church will enjoy God and heaven.

27.
Heaven in relation to hell

It was a spontaneous expression of surprise and also an encouragement. A teenage girl had spent some time relaxing in our home and before leaving she commented, 'You never shout in this house; it is so peaceful and loving.' I knew what she meant. Her own home was marred by quarrelling and bitterness; it was in sharp contrast to our home. At that moment, however, I caught a glimpse of heaven's perfect peace and happiness. While our family consists of growing but imperfect Christians, all the inhabitants of heaven are perfect and their relationships express completely the holy and loving character of God. In the absence of pain, death, sin, problems and disappointments, the happiness of Christians in heaven will be far superior even to the joy they experience in this world. Some of the important reasons why heaven is such a happy and perfect place have been given in the preceding chapters in this section. But the point needs to be emphasized that nothing unhappy can occur in heaven.

One lingering question, however, remains. What about those who suffer eternally in hell? How can Christians be happy knowing that these people are in such an awful place? This is the question we will attempt to answer in this chapter as we conclude the section on what heaven is like.

The biblical evidence

There is evidence in the Bible that the inhabitants of hell and heaven will be aware of, and even able to see, one another. One important line of evidence is found in Luke 16:19-31, where the Lord Jesus relates the story of Lazarus and the rich unbelieving man. Nowhere in his parables does the Lord give a name to any of the characters, as he does here. He also confines all his parables to events in this life alone. For these reasons this story cannot be regarded as a parable and he may well have been referring to two real persons who lived and died at that time. He is teaching here by way of analogy and drawing aside for us the curtain of mystery which clouds life after death.

What I want you to notice is the fact that the rich man 'was in torment' (v. 23) and from hell 'He looked up and saw Abraham far away, with Lazarus by his side.' Although the gulf between heaven and hell is unbridgeable, yet those in hell are aware of Christians in heaven. Furthermore, in verses 24-31 it is clear that Abraham knows about the fate of the rich man in hell and this suggests that the inhabitants of hell are visible to Christians in heaven or, at least, that they are aware of their being in hell.

There is more evidence. When the Lord Jesus returns in glory as King and Judge he will separate Christians and non-Christians (Matt. 25:31-33). To Christians he will say, 'Come, you who are blessed by my Father; take your inheritance, the kingdom prepared for you since the creation of the world' (v. 34). It appears that these Christians will also hear the Lord say to unbelievers, 'Depart from me, you who are cursed, into the eternal fire prepared for the devil and his angels' (v. 41). The inhabitants of heaven and hell will be aware of each other's destiny and reward.

Another line of evidence is found in Isaiah 66:22-24: ' "As the new heavens and the new earth that I make will endure before me," declares the LORD, "so will your name and your descendants endure. From one New Moon to another and from one Sabbath to another, all mankind will come and bow down before me," says the LORD. "And they will go out and look upon the dead bodies of those who rebelled against me; their worm will not die, nor will their fire be quenched, and they will be loathsome to all mankind." '

Some who teach the theory of annihilation or conditional immortality confine the end statement in this quotation (v. 24) to physical death and deny that it refers to an eternal state of suffering in hell.[1] But this statement in Isaiah cannot, and must not, be dismissed so easily and I submit three significant arguments in favour of its ultimate fulfilment in hell.

First of all, the context of these verses in Isaiah 66 is eschatological. Two truths are emphasized here. One is the glorious blessing and deliverance of God's people; the other is the judgement and punishment of unbelievers. It is true that the physical death of unbelievers is mentioned in the Isaiah text, but there is more. Beyond physical death, unbelievers will still suffer and the language of the 'worm' and the 'fire' points to this. Does the reference to the 'worm' point to guilty, tormented consciences? This eschatological perspective is confirmed in verse 22 with reference to 'the new heavens and the new earth', as well as the fact in verse 23 that 'All mankind will come and bow down before me.' Notice too, that both of these statements relate to the future.

Secondly, in the New Testament the apostle Peter refers to Isaiah's prophecy when he writes, 'We are looking forward to a new heaven and a new earth, the home of righteousness' (2 Peter 3:13). For Peter, this is without doubt eschatological for it is related to the return of the Lord Jesus Christ in glory (see vv. 4,10) when world history will end and the whole universe will be renewed.

Thirdly, the Lord himself quotes directly from this passage in Isaiah when describing the misery and torment of hell: 'Their worm does not die, and the fire is not quenched' (Mark 9:48; cf. Isa. 66:24). Our Lord uses the Greek word *Gehenna* ('hell') three times in verses 43, 45 and 47; the danger of being 'thrown into hell' (vv. 45,47) is an awful reality for people. 'Fire' in the context of hell refers to God's wrath upon sin: 'Our God is a consuming fire' (Heb. 12:29). Observe also how the Lord Jesus stresses twice in Mark chapter 9 that 'The fire never goes out' (vv. 44,48)[2] thus underlining the permanence both of divine wrath and the conscious punishment of unbelievers in hell.

The conclusion of Maurice Roberts in this respect is justified: 'Isaiah's words are surely meaningless if they do not teach that in heaven the redeemed will be able to see the damned in their torments. The redeemed shall see them, Isaiah declares, and there will be reaction in the redeemed in that they will "abhor" the wicked who are so suffering.'[3]

And from the different statements of Scripture we have already referred to, Jonathan Edwards affirms, 'The saints in heaven and the sinners in hell shall some way or other have a direct and immediate apprehension of each other's state.'[4]

How then can Christians be happy in heaven if they are continually aware of the sufferings of unbelievers in hell?

The main Bible answer is that Christians in heaven will be perfect like the Lord and will view everything from a divine, not a human perspective. That constitutes a major change for Christians. It is a fact that this perspective also belongs to Christians in this world but only to a limited degree and then it is often mixed with selfish and man-centred priorities. However, in heaven it will be different. No selfishness or sin will trouble Christians there. In fact, only the Lord will be important to them and they will be captivated by, and burn with love to, God. Their one passion will be the glory of God. Two passages in the book of Revelation illustrate the point well. In chapter 6 we see Christians in heaven; in the previous chapter they are described as worshipping but here they are also praying and longing. But for what? Verse 10 provides the answer: 'How long, Sovereign Lord, holy and true, until you judge the inhabitants of the earth and avenge our blood?' The prayer relates to the consummation of God's purposes in which the glory of God will be fully revealed and also acknowledged by all. This will include the resurrection of the dead, the submission and defeat of Christ's enemies, together with the punishment of all unbelievers in hell. In all these ways the Lord will display his holiness, justice and sovereignty; it is this desire for the honour of God and the display of his glorious character which will motivate Christians in heaven.

The other important reference is found in Revelation 19:1-3. Here the Lord is described as taking action against his enemies, including those who killed Christians. The response of the church in heaven is ecstatic and united. There was 'the roar of a great multitude' shouting:

'Hallelujah!
Salvation and glory and power belong to our God,
    for true and just are his judgements.
He has condemned the great prostitute
    who corrupted the earth by her adulteries.
He has avenged on her the blood of his servants.'

And again they shouted:

'Hallelujah!
The smoke from her goes up for ever and ever.'

To confirm the rightness of these holy desires in heaven, 'a voice came from the throne', saying:

> Praise our God,
>> all you his servants,
> you who fear him,
>> both small and great!

(Rev. 19:5).

The response of heaven's inhabitants grew louder, 'like loud peals of thunder' (v. 6). Earlier, in Revelation 18:20, the rejoicing of the church in heaven over its enemies is something which God required:

> Rejoice over her, O heaven!
>> Rejoice, saints and apostles and prophets!
> God has judged her for the way she treated you.

The conclusions we can draw from this evidence

In conclusion, we can make three observations on these scriptural statements.

First, *Christians in heaven will not be distressed by the sufferings of unbelievers in hell.* That is not due to insensitivity, selfishness or sinfulness on the part of Christians. Not at all, because their response to the sufferings of those in hell will be consistent with the response of God himself. Although it is difficult for us to appreciate the fact, in heaven Christians will only love what God loves and hate what God hates.

The second observation is that *Christians in heaven will actually rejoice in the divine justice* expressed in the punishment of unbelievers. Such rejoicing relates exclusively to the display and honouring of the glorious character of God.

Christians will not rejoice in the sufferings of unbelievers as such. They will rejoice only because such sufferings reveal and glorify the justice and wrath of God. There will be no pity shown by Christians to the sufferings of unbelievers in hell.

And, third, observe that the supreme reason for it is that *the glory of God will be the all-important consideration* for them. Jonathan Edwards expresses the point succinctly: 'Heaven will have no pity for hell, not because the saints are unloving, but because they are perfectly loving. They love as God loves and whom God loves, being now in perfect conformity with his love.'[5]

Here and now our duty is to love all people and to seek earnestly their salvation. Compassion on our part as Christians is essential. We must repent of our indifference. However, in heaven compassion gives way to love, love to God and a consuming passion for his glory as they identify themselves wholly with God. For this reason even the divine punishment of unbelievers in hell will stimulate rejoicing and praise from heaven's inhabitants because God is glorified in hell as well as in heaven. Yes, heaven will be perfectly happy despite the awareness of hell throughout eternity.

Section IV
Heaven: its challenge

28.
Reaching heaven

Will I get there? I did not think I would. And on a couple of occasions I nearly turned back. The occasion was a walk to the top of Wales's highest mountain, Snowdon, in the north-west of the country. At first the weather was warm and dry; all the teenagers in my group were keen to tackle the mountain. For the first hour or so it was fairly straightforward hill-walking and everyone seemed happy. Then it changed unexpectedly. The hill-walking became more demanding and steep; as we looked ahead at times, we could see the steep paths we still needed to climb. Low-level clouds appeared, quickly engulfing us in a steady drizzle of rain and a swirling mist. We were really in difficulties. Discouragement crept in, followed by complaints, and we all struggled to move forward. The vote to continue the walk, however, was unanimous and we agreed to encourage one another more for the rest of the walk. Feeling relieved and exhilarated, we eventually reached the summit although exhausted and thirsty.

Do you feel like that with regard to heaven? Does it seem like a summit far away which appears impossible for you to reach? Perhaps you are discouraged, weary and finding your circumstances too difficult to cope with. That has certainly been the experience of some Christians in the past as well as in the present.

Think, for example, of some famous Christian hymn-writers and their trials. Paul Gerhardt (1607-1676) was a member of the German Lutheran Church. For most of his life he faced many difficulties and trials. At one period he and his young family were made refugees and it was far from easy trusting God for accommodation, income and a job. Part of his life was spent witnessing the atrocities of the Thirty Years' War in Germany and only in 1657, at the age of forty-four, did he secure a permanent job when he was appointed minister of a church in Berlin. Only one of his five children survived childhood; then his wife suffered a long illness from which she died in 1666. His remaining years were spent in extremely pressurized and lonely circumstances. Some of his parishioners added to his burdens by opposing his useful, Christ-centred ministry. Gerhardt's last dying words were:

> Him no death has power to kill,
> But from many a dreaded ill
> Bears his spirit safe away.[1]

The words apply, of course, to all Christians and Gerhardt, despite having had so many discouragements, reached heaven safely.

Joseph Hart (1712-1768) was born in London to good Christian parents. However, from the age of twenty-one to forty-five he experienced considerable anxiety concerning his relationship to God and struggled profoundly with his own personal sin. A sermon in 1757 was the means of delivering and blessing him with a deep assurance of his personal salvation in Christ. Hart became a zealous Christian and then a useful minister of an independent church for the remaining eight years of his life. His own inward struggles and periods of darkness were many although the Lord gradually gave him a measure of victory and encouragement. Towards the end of his life, Hart remarked honestly, 'I confess myself a sinner still, and though I am not much tempted to outward gross acts of iniquity, yet inward corruptions and spiritual wickedness continually harass and perplex my soul and often make me cry out, "O wretched man that I am! Who shall deliver me from the body of this death?" '[2] Despite all his struggles, he too, reached heaven.

Now Paul Gerhardt and Joseph Hart are representative of many Christians over the centuries who experienced great personal hardships and conflict but still got to heaven. The apostolic exhortation to early Christians in the first century applies to all generations: 'We must go through many hardships to enter the kingdom of God' (Acts 14:22).

It is appropriate for us to probe the matter further and ask an important question: namely, how can Christians be so sure that they will reach heaven? The major answer to this question is that the Bible assures them of the fact and we can now briefly sample these Bible statements on the subject.

An important statement is recorded in John 6:37-40. The immediate context in verse 36 refers to those Jews who had seen and heard Jesus' teaching about salvation; they had also witnessed his miracles, yet had not believed. Would this jeopardize God's plan to save sinners? Not at all. 'All that the Father gives me,' insists the Lord Jesus, 'will come to me' (v. 37). Salvation does not depend on the whims of people, but on the sovereign decision and power of God. Jesus is confident that the Father will achieve his saving purposes. Those chosen by the Father (see also Eph. 1:4; Rom. 9:14-24) and given to Jesus that he should die for them 'will come to me'. There is no ambiguity or uncertainty about it. God will ensure the success of his plans.

The complementary truth is: 'And whoever comes to me I will never drive away.' The word translated 'drive away' refers to those individuals who are already 'in' a safe place. The

Lord Jesus, therefore, says of these Christians that 'I will certainly keep [them] in.'[3] Not only, then, are Christians received and welcomed by Christ, but they are also preserved by him.

The reason for this preservation and safekeeping of Christians is stated in verses 38-40. The reason is a powerful one indeed and relates, first of all, to the Lord's mission from heaven to earth which involved only doing his Father's will (v. 38). And that will of the Father is expressed in a twofold way: 'that I should lose none of all that he has given me, but raise them up at the last day' (v. 39). Each Christian must be kept in grace; then eventually even their bodies will also be resurrected 'at the last day'. This is repeated in verse 40 with the emphasis that Christians 'shall have eternal life'. There is no possibility of their failing to reach heaven.

Another helpful statement by the Lord Jesus is recorded in John 10:28-30. Verse 27 identifies two essential characteristics of Christians: they 'listen' to Christ as he speaks in the Bible and, secondly, they 'follow' and obey him in their lives. To such people, the Lord Jesus affirms, 'I give them eternal life' (v. 28). He then adds a statement underlining his own absolute power and the fact that Christians are guaranteed to reach heaven: 'No one can snatch them out of my hand.' To show the complete impossibility of Christians failing to reach heaven, we are told in verse 29 that the security provided by Jesus the Good Shepherd is also supported by God the Father: 'No one can snatch them out of my Father's hand.' No one and nothing can isolate Christians from this firm divine grip upon them; they will all reach heaven safely.

I have concentrated on these two statements by Jesus Christ in John's Gospel because of their importance and clarity, but it must be remembered that there are many other statements in the Bible assuring us that all Christians will reach heaven. For example, the apostle Peter informs Christians that an inheritance is 'kept in heaven for you'. In addition, Christians themselves 'are shielded by God's power' until heaven is reached or the Lord Jesus returns in glory 'in the last time' (1 Peter 1:4,5). A similar triumphant note is struck by the apostle Paul when he declares that nothing at all 'will be able to separate us from the love of God that is in Christ Jesus our Lord' (Rom. 8:39).

You may recall that we are answering the question posed earlier in the chapter — namely, how can Christians be so certain that they will arrive safely in heaven? The major answer is that the Bible itself in its teaching assures them of the fact, and that is why we have mentioned some references like John chapters 6 and 10. One further answer can be mentioned here briefly and that is that the Holy Spirit through the Bible gives to individual Christians an inward, sometimes strong, assurance that they are the children of God and destined for glory.

Assurance means being convinced as Christians that the Lord has saved us and will take us to heaven, but this true assurance follows or accompanies trust in Jesus Christ as Saviour and Lord. As we have seen, this assurance is strengthened by the Bible as we believe and embrace its teaching for ourselves. But there is more. The Holy Spirit who dwells and works in each Christian bears an inward testimony that the individual is adopted into God's family and is an heir of eternal life. The apostle Paul expresses this in Romans 8:15-17: 'For you did not receive a spirit that makes you a slave again to fear, but you received the Spirit of sonship. And by him we cry, "*Abba*, Father." The Spirit himself testifies with our spirit that we are God's children. Now if we are children, then we are heirs — heirs of God and co-heirs with Christ, if indeed we share in his sufferings in order that we may also share in his glory.' The Holy Spirit, then, can give a conviction or certainty to individual Christians that they are the Lord's and bound for heaven. But this inward witness by the Spirit must also be accompanied by 'the fruit of the Spirit' which results in moral change and godly character. This fruit 'is love, joy, peace, patience, kindness, goodness, faithfulness, gentleness and self-control' (Gal. 5:22-23). Such Christians have a well-grounded assurance that they are the Lord's and that their destiny is heaven.

In the next chapter we will continue this theme further and suggest further guarantees why all Christians will reach heaven.

29.
Reaching heaven: guaranteed for all Christians

Guaranteed to reach heaven — that is what the Bible promises to all Christians, and only to Christians. In the previous chapter we considered certain aspects of this guarantee but in this chapter I intend to provide an overview in order to show how extensive and reliable this divine guarantee really is. If you are a genuine Christian, there is no need for you to fear that you will miss out on heaven. Your fears and doubts have no solid foundation. But how reliable and effective is this guarantee which the Lord gives in the Bible about heaven? The question will be answered now in three related ways from the Bible.

God the Father

In the Holy Trinity the three divine persons, Father, Son and Holy Spirit, are together and unitedly responsible for the salvation of the elect; each person is equal and fully committed to the divine plan of salvation. However, within the economy of the Holy Trinity the Bible ascribes particular functions, in the planning, accomplishment and application of salvation, to each divine person. The tasks are shared out, yet there is perfect co-operation and unity in all that they do. Notice that the Father is represented as planning salvation and sending the

Son to achieve it, while the Holy Spirit was sent by the Father and Son to apply this salvation to sinners. It is encouraging that in order to save the elect the divine persons in the blessed Holy Trinity shared the work and responsibilities among themselves. One famous preacher put it like this: 'The Son has put Himself at the disposal of the Father, and the Spirit has put Himself at the disposal of the Father and the Son. The Spirit does not speak of Himself, but received His words and His works from the Father, though He was equal and eternal — the economic Trinity. So that while, in a sense, we can say that it was the Father who sent the Son, and the Son who came and did the work, and the Spirit applied it, we must at the same time say this: God was in it all.'[1]

At this point we are interested in showing how the Father's work helps to guarantee that all Christians will arrive safely in heaven. The crucial point to grasp is that ultimately reaching heaven depends on God rather than on the individual. True Christians have responsibilities to obey, use the means of grace appointed for their spiritual nourishment and persevere believingly despite discouragements and temptations. It is also true that Christians can fall into sins, grieve the Holy Spirit, bring dishonour to the church, as well as to the Lord's name, and also incur chastening. Nevertheless, if they are among the elect they 'can neither totally nor finally fall away from the state of grace; but shall certainly persevere therein to the end, and be eternally saved'. The *Westminster Confession of Faith* continues: 'This perseverance of the saints depends not upon their own free will, but upon the immutability of the decree of election, flowing from the free and unchangeable love of God the Father...'[2]

This teaching concerning the Father's electing grace is foundational to our theme in this chapter. He decreed all that would happen in history, yet without instigating or encouraging sin. However, in such decrees he also respects the free agency of people. 'The Lord reigns' (Ps. 97:1) is the consistent emphasis of the Bible; he rules over everything and everyone (see Dan. 4:35, Eph. 1:11). One glorious aspect of his eternal decrees is that the Father has himself chosen those individuals who are to be saved. The following statements in the Bible confirm the fact beyond question:

> At that time Jesus said, 'I praise you, Father, Lord of heaven and earth, because you have hidden these things from the wise and learned, and revealed them to little children. Yes, Father, for this was your good pleasure' (Matt. 11:25-26).

> And all who were appointed for eternal life believed (Acts 13:48).

> Therefore God has mercy on whom he wants to have mercy, and he hardens whom he wants to harden (Rom. 9:18; see also vv. 10-25).

> From the beginning God chose you to be saved through the sanctifying work of the Spirit and through belief in the truth (2 Thess. 2:13).

This fact is consistently taught in the Bible: God the Father chooses those who will be saved. Christians may have many unresolved questions in their minds until they reach heaven but their responsibility is to accept what the Bible teaches and acknowledge that he has the absolute right to deal with people as he pleases. A person is a Christian because God decided that he or she would be. This fact should comfort Christians greatly. His decision is an eternal one; it is *unconditional* in that it is not subject to any conditions or merit on the part of people. It is also an *unchangeable* decision, for he will not change his mind concerning the elect nor allow them to be lost. He guarantees their arrival in heaven.

God the Son

The great plan of salvation, including the choice of sinners to be saved, is achieved only in and through the Lord Jesus Christ. But the question arises: how does Christ's unique role in salvation contribute to the divine guarantee that all Christians reach heaven safely? I want to refer to just a few of the ways in which Christ's role is crucial for the Christian's safe entry to heaven.

1. The adequacy of his sacrifice for the elect

The guilt, power, punishment and pollution of their sin were all dealt with decisively and fully in Christ's death on the cross. For example, 'Christ redeemed us from the curse of the law by becoming a curse for us,' writes the apostle Paul (Gal. 3:13). Jesus Christ redeemed his people by becoming a curse in their place and that is why on the cross their punishment and curse were transferred to him as their substitute. He was also their 'propitiation' (Rom. 3:25, AV) for in his sacrifice he bore the full weight of God's wrath and turned it away from the elect. For him it meant being forsaken by God, unimaginable sorrow, punishment and physical death; for Christians it means safety and eternal salvation. Spurgeon's observation is accurate and helpful: 'Christ so died that he infallibly secured the salvation of a multitude that no man can number, who through Christ's death not only may be saved, but are saved, must be saved, and cannot by any possibility run the hazard of being anything but saved.'[3] His sacrifice was adequate indeed and guarantees that the elect will reach heaven.

2. The acceptance of his sacrifice by the Father

Besides vindicating his teaching and constituting a glorious victory over sin, death and hell as well as Satan, the resurrection of Jesus on the third day was also proof that God the Father had accepted his sacrifice for sin. Here is the ultimate proof that Jesus' sacrifice for the elect was accepted by the Father. Christ's work was not only finished; it also met with the approval of heaven and guarantees the justification of believers before a holy God (Rom. 4:25). But not only was Jesus raised from the dead, he also ascended to the Father in heaven, where he rules with absolute power over the universe. It is from this position of authority that the Lord Jesus builds and protects his church and provides for and blesses Christians (Acts 2:33; John 16:7-15). He guarantees that the elect will reach heaven.

3. The authority of the Lord's prayers for the elect

Exalted at the right hand of God the Father, the Lord '… is also interceding for us' (Rom. 8:34). In the letter to the Hebrews we are told that 'Because Jesus lives for ever, he has a permanent priesthood. Therefore he is able to save completely those who come to God through him, because he *always lives to intercede for them*' (Heb. 7:24-25, italics mine).

His prayers for the elect are effective and comprehensive as well as personal. Recently I heard an encouraging report of a Protestant church in Western Europe. The church has grown over the past fourteen years from twenty-four to over three hundred members and still people are being converted and added to that church. The minister explained in detail what had happened. He described himself as an ordinary preacher; no gimmicks or campaigns had been used. In fact the emphasis had been on regular Sunday preaching services, group and one-to-one Bible studies in the week, prayer meetings, holiness of life and personal evangelism. And God blessed the work. However, the minister identified the main reason for the growth. He attributed it to the sovereign God who had constrained and enabled a group of men in the church to pray together for the locality every Friday evening for over fifty years. They were young converts when they first covenanted to pray together and now, though some have died, the members of the group are all over seventy years of age and continue to meet together for prayer on Fridays. God is answering their prayers. But if the prayers of Christians are answered, how much more the prayers of the Lord Jesus for his church! After all, Christ prays for those whom the Father also loves and chooses. Christ died for these too and purchased their eternal salvation. His prayers for Christians, therefore, are always effective; it is these prayers which also guarantee that all the elect will reach heaven.

4. The advantages of the union of Christians with Christ

A further point must also be made. Elected by the Father in Christ from eternity and redeemed by the blood of Christ, the elect are brought out of their sinful condition by the inward supernatural work of the Holy Spirit in them. They are drawn effectually to Christ, then intimately and mystically united to Christ. This union between Christians and Christ is a loving as well as a mystical and fruitful one; it is strong and eternal. Because Christ the Head lives, Christians live also eternally and draw on Christ's life and resources while in this world. Nothing can destroy this union or prevent the Christian from reaching heaven. Christ himself sustains, quickens and keeps the elect (see, e.g. John 15:1-7; Eph. 4:16; Col. 2:6-7).

God the Holy Spirit

The Spirit's work in the elect also guarantees their safe arrival in heaven. In giving spiritual life and light to individuals, the Holy Spirit proceeds to lead them to Jesus Christ. In each Christian, and in fact the whole church of Christ, it is true that 'God's Spirit lives in you' (1 Cor. 3:16). His work is to make Christians holy and to give them strength to fight against sin as well as to persevere in obedience and faith. Without the ongoing assistance and quickening of the Holy Spirit, Christians would be unable to overcome sin and the world; with the Holy Spirit, however, they will be prepared for heaven and preserved until they reach that glorious place. Whatever is against them, Christians will overcome in the power of the Holy Spirit.

John Bunyan illustrates the point well in his *Pilgrim's Progress*. He pictures Christian being led by Interpreter to a place where a fire was burning against a wall with a person alongside continually throwing a lot of water on the fire in order to put it out. The remarkable thing was that, despite all the water being poured on it, the fire burned 'higher and hotter'. Christian was then given an explanation by Interpreter. The fire represented God's work of grace in the heart of the Christian and the one throwing water on the fire to put it out represents the devil. To explain why the fire was burning more brightly, Christian was told to look at the other side of the wall, where he saw a man continually pouring oil on the fire. Interpreter then explained that the man with oil represents Christ, 'who continually with the oil of his grace maintains the work already begun in the heart...'[4] Yes, Christians are sustained, blessed and preserved until they reach heaven.

For all these reasons, and the covenant of grace sealed with the blood of Christ, the elect will all arrive in glory. It is guaranteed — by God.

30.
Heaven: living under its rule

As we have seen in the last two chapters, all Christians are guaranteed to reach heaven by the grace and power of God. No Christian can be lost. On the other hand, those who are going to heaven should live in this world as citizens of heaven. Christians in their lives here must be other-worldly, or heavenly-minded, in all they do and say. In contrast to unbelievers, whose 'destiny is destruction, their god is their stomach, and their glory is in their shame' and whose 'mind is on earthly things', the apostle Paul tells the Philippian Christians, 'But our citizenship is in heaven' (Phil. 3:19,20). The word 'citizenship' means 'homeland' or 'commonwealth' and for all Christians, therefore, their 'homeland' is heaven. This means that they follow the rules of heaven and seek to live in accordance with the standards of heaven. Their future is in heaven, but on earth they live as strangers and pilgrims (Heb. 11:13; 1 Peter 2:11). In this chapter I want to remind Christians of their responsibility to live here under the rule of heaven and this responsibility can be expressed in two ways.

Priority

Most people have to respect priorities in their lives. For example, a housewife gives priority to preparing food for the family rather than shopping for pleasure or visiting a friend for coffee. A young child needs to be collected from school, or taken for swimming or music lessons, so the parent has to interrupt other duties in order to give priority to the child. If you are like myself, you juggle with different priorities daily in an attempt to do what is essential and helpful.

Similarly, the Bible makes it clear that Christians have priorities, in fact absolute priorities, to please and obey the Lord. Our Lord Jesus Christ makes the point abundantly clear in the Sermon on the Mount in Matthew's Gospel, chapters 5-7. In this section the Lord indicates in detail how Christians should behave in this world as members of his heavenly kingdom. One such example is when he says, 'But seek first his kingdom and his righteousness, and all these things will be given to you as well' (Matt. 6:33). Rather than worrying about the basic necessities of life, the first priority of Christians is to please God by constantly doing what he commands. This must come 'first' and above everything else in their lives. Abraham illustrates this priority when he obeyed God's call to leave home. Solomon's priority in asking for wisdom as king, rather than for personal wealth or pleasure, is a further example of this principle. Similarly, the apostle Paul states that 'For to me to live is Christ' (Phil. 1:21) rather than self, pleasure or fame.

The point is made in a different way by the apostle Paul in Romans 12:1-2. In view of God's glorious salvation, the apostle informs us that Christians need to be wholly committed to God, in body and soul. Here he appeals to them to offer their bodies 'as living sacrifices, holy and pleasing to God' (v. 1). Against the background of animal sacrifices at that time, the exhortation was meaningful. Christians, too, must be wholly given to the Lord and their bodies used to obey as well as serve the Lord. Verse 2 indicates that Christians should not be moulded by the attitudes and standards of unbelieving people in the world; they should be 'transformed by the renewing of your mind', that is, thinking in a biblical and radically different way from that of unbelievers. Such radical thinking involves priorities — God first in all things. Is this true of you? It is not enough to admire famous Christians and missionaries for their sacrificial obedience to the Lord, for the same biblical priorities which governed their lives and thinking apply to all Christians everywhere.

Perspective

The *Concise Oxford Dictionary* informs us that a perspective is 'a mental view of the relative importance of things',[1] and for Christians this is determined by the Bible. There is one biblical perspective which is relevant to our theme at this point and that is the perspective of eternity. The apostle Paul uses this perspective frequently, as do other New Testament writers, and his words in 2 Corinthians 4:17-18 are helpful in this respect: 'For our light and momentary troubles are achieving for us an eternal glory that far outweighs them all. So we fix our eyes not on what is seen, but on what is unseen. For what is seen is temporary, but what is unseen is eternal.'

Paul had many hardships and troubles, some of which are referred to earlier in the chapter (vv. 8-12). He does not complain about them but views them in the light of eternity. From that perspective his problems are regarded as being 'light and momentary'. Then he explains how he is able to keep this eternal perspective: 'So we fix our eyes not on what is seen, but on what is unseen.'

And he uses two different Greek verbs in verse 18 to make his point. The first word is helpfully translated in the NIV as 'fix our eyes', that is, to concentrate one's attention on a matter, to watch carefully and to be fully absorbed with it, just as a competent driver concentrates fully on his driving. But the apostle Paul commands the Christian not to concentrate attention wholly on things which are 'seen', such as buildings, health, business, money, problems, pleasure, or even family. Such matters must not be neglected, of course, but they must not be given supreme importance in our lives. Our eyes ought to be fixed 'on what is unseen', that is, God, the glorious gospel and heaven.

The second Greek verb is translated as 'seen' and consists of a mere glance or a more general look at what is 'seen', namely, his troubles as well as other worldly concerns. By contrast, like Paul, Christians are to fix their eyes on the 'unseen' spiritual and eternal perspective which finds its consummation in heaven.

An illustration is appropriate at this point. In January 1957 five missionaries, all young married men, were killed by Auca Indians in South America as they endeavoured to reach that primitive tribe with the gospel of Christ. After receiving news that their husbands had been killed, the widows were flown over their husbands' graves. From the small aeroplane they were able to see the white sand and the clearly marked graves. These wives were shocked, upset and lonely, but as Christians they knew peace as they submitted to the Lord's will. There was no bitterness or resentment. Alongside their deep sense of loss, however, there was an eternal perspective which shone brightly through their sorrow. As one wife, for example, looked down from the aeroplane on those graves, she recalled the words of Scripture: 'absent from the body, present with the Lord' (2 Cor. 5:8, AV). The wives knew that the men were in heaven and this biblical perspective sustained and encouraged them in their bereavement. This is part of what it means to fix our eyes on what is unseen.

Another aspect of this eternal perspective can be mentioned briefly as we conclude the chapter. One aspect of living under heaven's rule in this life is that Christians are accountable to Christ. Their salvation, of course, is not in question. While we all deserve to go to hell because 'The wages of sin is death' (Rom. 6:23), the astonishing news is that God 'does not treat us as our sins deserve or repay us according to our iniquities' (Ps. 103:10). But God does this by grace alone. That is the glorious gospel of Christ. 'Grace' means it is completely undeserved; it is free, wholly from God and without any human contribution or merit.[2]

However, all Christians remain accountable to Christ; their lives and work must one day bear the gaze and scrutiny of Christ their Lord and Judge. Many Christians in the history of the church have been profoundly aware of this awesome fact. For example, George Whitefield was greatly used by God in the eighteenth-century revival in England and America. His ministry, nevertheless, although powerful and fruitful, was opposed by some of the clergy in a number of ways.

One example became known as the 'St Margaret's Church' incident. This preaching incident was distorted by critics to suggest that in 1739 Whitefield had forced his way into the church pulpit to preach. The story had been fabricated by his enemies, but one of Whitefield's friends, who had been present in St Margaret's Church and witnessed all that happened, replied to critics in order to establish the actual facts. Although shaken by the criticism and lies, Whitefield wrote in his *Journal*: 'Thou shalt answer for me, my Lord and my God. A little while and we shall appear at the judgement seat of Christ. Then shall my innocence be made clear as the light and my dealings as the noonday.'[3]

Later in 1739 Whitefield wrote to a magistrate in Basingstoke who had criticized his preaching meeting in the area as being schismatic and riotous. He concluded his letter: 'As for judging me, to my own Master I stand or fall. At His dreadful tribunal I will meet you; and then you shall see what is in the heart of, honoured sir, your very humble servant.'[4]

For Whitefield, it was a fact: one day, he and other people would stand before Christ as Judge. Whether it was the vindication of his motives, establishing facts, or scrutinizing the quality of his ministry, Whitefield knew that these things would occur at the last day when all will appear before the judgement seat of Christ. And that is taught in the New Testament.

Consider the apostle Paul's exhortation to preachers: 'But each one should be careful how he builds… If any man builds on this foundation using gold, silver, costly stones, wood, hay or straw, his work will be shown for what it is, because the Day will bring it to light' (1 Cor. 3:10,12-13). The apostle, urging faithful stewardship to Christ, declares later his relative indifference to human judgements passed on him. 'My conscience is clear,' he writes, 'but that does not make me innocent. It is the Lord who judges me. Therefore judge nothing before the appointed time; wait till the Lord comes. He will bring to light what is hidden in darkness and will expose the motives of men's hearts. At that time each will receive his praise from God' (1 Cor. 4:4-5).

The practical implications of this eternal perspective are enormous and far-reaching. Christians need to live and work here as those who will give an account of themselves and their stewardship to Christ the righteous Judge. 'For we must all appear before the judgement seat of Christ,' adds the apostle Paul, 'that each one may receive what is due to him for the things done while in the body, whether good or bad' (2 Cor. 5:10). Admittedly, some Christians are uncertain concerning the interpretation and significance of these statements quoted from 1 Corinthians 3-4 as well as from 2 Corinthians 5:10. And some, like myself, are unsure whether the Bible teaches degrees of rewards in heaven for Christians or not. Nevertheless, these differences concerning the subject should not cloud the fact that Christians are accountable to Christ and will be scrutinized, recognized and praised by Christ on his return in glory. Should this not stimulate Christians to live more carefully and biblically under the authority of the one before whom they will appear? In an appendix, I examine in detail the subject of degrees of rewards for Christians in heaven. Although the treatment is not exhaustive, I trust it will stimulate those interested to reflect further on the subject.

Before concluding this chapter, I want to underline the accountability of Christians by referring to Joni Eareckson Tada's book, *Heaven: what will it be like?*[5] Joni talks about the judgement seat of Christ briefly over three pages but rightly rejects the suggestion that it is a trial to establish the guilt or innocence of Christians. 'It is more like a judging stand,' she explains, 'to ascertain your capacity to serve God.'[6] An analogy is then used by Joni in which she pictures a judge's stand at a housing contractors' convention where rewards are given to all the architects, builders, foremen and construction teams. The quality of their work is inspected individually and each one receives praise, not condemnation, for their share of work. Joni pictures the praise given to some individuals as being greater than that given to others but each person receives his reward. As a prize, the judge is pictured as saying, 'Well done! You have accomplished much with these few buildings, now we will put you in charge of a big development.' The builders and others then tackle their new assignment with great enthusiasm. 'Each one,' writes Joni, 'walks away from the convention happy, heartened and with an increased capacity to serve the industry.'[7] The analogy has its weaknesses but aspects of it, and Joni's application, are helpful. Christians in this life have the responsibility to love and serve God well, using building materials which will have eternal value. 'Every day,' she insists, 'we have the opportunity to … apply our energies toward building something that lasts…' Christ will scrutinize the quality of the work and lives of Christians. It is a challenge. This eternal perspective should permeate and control all that Christians think, desire, say and do.

31.
Heaven: crossing the river

John Bunyan describes vividly and allegorically the final stage in the journey of Christian to heaven, the Celestial City. Christian and his companion, Hopeful, had arrived in close proximity to the city and enjoyed a much better view of it. As they came closer, the reflection of the sun on the city made it so bright and glorious that they were unable to look on it directly with the naked eye. Between heaven's entrance and themselves the two pilgrims saw a river, but there was no bridge to cross the deep river. They were informed that it was necessary to go through the river to reach the gate of the Celestial City.

Entering the water, Christian was alarmed as he felt himself sinking, but Hopeful encouraged him: 'Be of good cheer, my brother, I feel the bottom and it is good.' Sorrow, darkness and horror overwhelmed Christian but Hopeful struggled to keep his brother's head above the water. 'Brother, I see the gate, and men standing by to receive us,' were Hopeful's comforting words to his companion. Other reassurances were given to show that God had not forsaken Christian and, finally, Hopeful added the words: 'Be of good cheer, Jesus Christ maketh thee whole.'

Immediately Christian himself shouted excitedly, 'Oh, I see him again! and he tells me, "When thou passest through the water, I will be with thee, and through the rivers, they shall not overflow thee." '

Quite soon Christian felt firm ground under his feet again and, with his companion, reached the other side of the river. They were escorted up a hill, left their 'mortal garments' behind and heard about the glories of the city they were entering. The city's beauty was inexpressible, the conditions perfect and the privileges unimaginable.

How glorious is the city of heaven? 'You are going now,' the two pilgrims were told, 'to the Paradise of God ... you shall have white robes given you, and your walk and talk shall be every day with the King, even all the days of eternity ... you shall not see again such things as ... sorrow, sickness, affliction and death...'

Both Christian and Hopeful asked what they themselves had to do in such a glorious place and they were informed: 'You must there receive the comfort of all your toil and have joy for all your sorrow; you must reap what you have sown ... wear crowns of gold and enjoy the perpetual sight and vision of the Holy One ... serve him continually... There your eyes shall be delighted with seeing, and your ears with hearing the pleasant voice of the Mighty One ... enjoy your friends again...'

As the two men approached heaven's gate, angels met them and shouted, 'Blessed are they that are called to the Marriage Supper of the Lamb.' Then several of the King's trumpeters arrived who gave them 'ten thousand welcomes'. Their music was 'melodious' and, with all that they saw, it was 'as if heaven itself was come down to meet them. As they entered through the gate of heaven the city bells rang for joy and the men were told: "Enter ye into the joy of our Lord," then they themselves sang loudly, "Blessing, honour, glory, and power be to him that sits on the throne and to the Lamb, for ever and ever." ' Christian and his companion had reached heaven safely.[1]

Bunyan's description of heaven and Christian's entry to that glorious place is only an allegory, but it is firmly grounded in, and full of references from, the Bible. However, it is not

Bunyan's masterly description of heaven I want to focus on in this chapter, but rather the river of death which Bunyan rightly reminds us needs to be crossed by Christians before they enter heaven. What I want to do in the remainder of this chapter is to refer to the experience of some Christians as they faced death and prepared themselves to enter heaven. Although the choice of Christians to sample in this context is embarrassingly rich and extensive, I am confining myself to some less famous names.

Bunyan himself died in 1688 after a life of trials and hardships. We know little about his last days except that he travelled on horseback from Reading to London in heavy, driving rain. He preached a couple of days later to a large crowd, then developed a high fever. For ten days before his death he was desperately ill. Occasionally he spoke brief but helpful words to people around him. He died quietly yet triumphantly on 31 August, just prior to his sixtieth birthday. He crossed the river of death.

In facing death, the Lord graciously assists and blesses Christians as the following examples indicate.

Thomas Hog was a Scottish Covenant preacher born, like Bunyan, in 1628. Devoted to Christ and the Bible, Hog was at times arrested and imprisoned for his faith. He died in 1691 after being sustained by the Lord in his illness. On one occasion a person observed the pain he suffered and Hog replied, 'For a hundred and a hundred times my Lord has assured me that I shall be with him for ever, but I am making moan for my body.' He longed to go to heaven and remarked, 'Pity me, O my friends, and do not pray for my life. Allow me to go to my eternal rest.' As death approached, Hog was greatly comforted by the Bible and the Lord's presence with him. 'Never did the sun shine more brightly ... than Christ, the Sun of Righteousness, hath shined on my soul,' he testified. Even in considerable pain and weakness he bore testimony that 'The unchangeableness of God is my rock.' As he lay dying, Hog remarked, 'Now he is come, he is come, my Lord is come! Praises, praises to him for evermore.'[2]

Similarly, Edward Payson died well as a Christian in 1827. Known for his prayerfulness and powerful preaching, Payson knew many pressures, as well as ill-health and depression. Just four weeks prior to his death he declared, 'Last night I had a full clear view of death as the king of terrors... But I had nothing to do with this... I felt that death was disarmed of all its terrors; all he could do was to touch me and let my soul loose to go to my Saviour.'[3] Despite growing physical weakness, his joy and experience of the Lord increased continually. 'If my happiness continues to increase,' he declared, 'I cannot support it much longer.' And referring to Bunyan's description of heaven and its glories, Payson added, 'Now my own experience has convinced me of it, and it infinitely transcends all my previous conceptions.' To his sister about a month before his death, Payson wrote, 'The celestial city is full in my view. Its glories beam upon me, its breezes fan me ... and its spirit is breathed into my heart. Nothing separates me from it but the river of death ... that may be crossed at a single step, whenever God shall give permission. The Sun of Righteousness has been gradually drawing nearer and nearer...'[4] After bidding farewell to his family, his final words included 'Peace! Peace! Victory! Victory!' and he added, 'I am going well, but God will surely be with you.'

The Methodist preacher William Bramwell also knew, like Payson, the Lord's victory and grace in dying. Bramwell seemed to sense in 1815 that he would die suddenly and soon. He also had some deep experiences of God at this time: 'My soul has experienced such a fellowship with God and heavenly things, as I never felt before. O the glory which shall be prevailed! I am swallowed up in him!'[5] To a friend he shared how he felt: 'I am always waiting to leave this body, that we may be clothed upon with our house in heaven. Glorious company!

Glorious place! I long, I wait for his coming!' He died suddenly and triumphantly in 1818.

Adoniram Judson was amongst the earliest missionary recruits to leave North America in the nineteenth century for overseas missionary work. Judson went to Burma where he preached the gospel for many years and translated the Scriptures. At the end of his life he grew so weak that his wife Emily wanted Adoniram to understand how near to death he might be. His reply expressed a strong faith: 'Death will never take me by surprise… I feel so strong in Christ. He has not led me so tenderly thus far, to forsake me at the very gate of heaven.' He continued, 'Yet when Christ calls me home, I shall go with the gladness of a boy bounding away from his school.'[6] Weeks later, in April 1850, the Lord called him home to heaven.

Prior to, and following, the 1940-1945 World War, Isobel Kuhn and her husband were missionaries on the China-Burma border, then later in Thailand with the China Inland Mission (now renamed Overseas Missionary Fellowship). They did valuable cross-cultural pioneering evangelism for the Lord during those years. It was during Isobel's first trip in search of the tribes of North Thailand that she was suddenly struck in the breast by a stick as the missionaries walked in single file along a jungle mountain path. A few months later walking the hills back to their base camp, Isobel had a fall caused by the slippery, wet surface. Strangely, she fell on a jagged stump and received a nasty blow in the same place as before. Preliminary medical tests reassured Isobel but a year later she discovered an abnormality in that same area of her body. Once again medical tests were negative, but after an operation Isobel eventually received news that she had a fast-growing malignant tumour and was given only a year to live, as there were also traces of secondary tumours in her chest.

The couple were flown back to the United States of America and friends provided a comfortable flat for their home. Isobel Kuhn prepared herself to cross the river of death. She quoted words written by a Christian worker: 'I cannot reach my home in that city of gold without passing through this dark valley of shadows. But I am not afraid, because the best Friend I ever had went through the same valley, long, long ago and drove away all its gloom. He has stuck by me through thick and thin since we first became acquainted fifty-five years ago and I hold His promise in printed form never to forsake me nor leave me alone. He will be with me as I walk through the valley of shadows, and I shall not lose my way when He is with me.'[7]

Was Isobel depressed about the nearness of death? 'Facing the end of one's earthly pilgrimage,' she insisted, 'is not a melancholy thing for a Christian. It is like preparation for the most exciting journey of all.'[8] Isobel prepared herself for that exciting journey and the Lord gave her peace as well as the sense of his presence during those final weeks. 'The platform of a dread disease,' she wrote just before her death, 'becomes but a springboard for heaven.'[9]

His grace is sufficient at all times. And the testimony of the Bible and of Christians throughout the history of the church is that the Lord gives grace to his people enabling them to face death. He is with the Christian in life and in dying. He tells his people:

> Fear not, for I have redeemed you;
>   I have summoned you by name; you are mine.
> When you pass through the waters,
>   I will be with you;
> and when you pass through the rivers,
>   they will not sweep over you
>
>   (Isa. 43:2).

With this assurance, Samuel Rutherford, the Scottish Covenanter, wrote in 1631 a letter to Lady Kenmure, who herself had experienced considerable sorrow in her family. In his letter he wrote these memorable words: 'Be content to wade through the waters betwixt [i.e. between] you and glory with Him, holding His hand fast, for He knoweth all the fords ... weary not; ... when ye are got up thither ... ye shall then say, "Four-and-twenty hours' abode in this place is worth threescore and ten years' sorrow upon earth."' [10]

A few weeks before his death, one of the desires on the heart of Martyn Lloyd-Jones was that he should have an 'abundant entrance' (2 Peter 1:11, AV) into the everlasting kingdom. He asked a close friend who visited him one day to pray for this as he wanted to die 'in the full sail of faith'. By the Lord's grace, he went safely through the rivers of physical weakness and death and had an 'abundant entrance' into heaven. [11]

The river must be crossed but the Lord is there to take Christians into that glorious country of heaven.

32.
Will I meet you in heaven?

That precise question had considerable significance for a young Scotsman several decades ago. And the story associated with it is interesting and also challenging. Born in 1933 in Ardnamurchan, Argyll, Douglas MacMillan was taught the Christian faith thoroughly by his parents and had the privilege of their godly example. As a teenager, however, he rebelled against Christianity and was fascinated by atheism and communism. His life became very worldly. It was in the final year of his mother's life that the young man began to be profoundly challenged concerning his relationship to God.

Returning home very late one evening after attending a dance, he heard his parents singing verses from a psalm. In her illness his mother was singing softly but triumphantly about her Lord. The young man was overcome and, instead of going into the house, he walked towards the nearby hills and wept.

Only a few weeks later he offered to read the Bible to his mother; she chose John chapter 14. He read the opening verses: 'Let not your heart be troubled: ye believe in God, believe also in me. In my Father's house are many mansions: if it were not so, I would have told you. I go to prepare a place for you. And if I go and prepare a place for you, I will come again, and receive you unto myself; that where I am, there ye may be also' (vv. 1-3, AV).

The mother beckoned to indicate that she did not want to hear any more verses in the chapter and the young man was surprised, insisting that he could read the whole chapter for her. But his mother had something else on her mind and wanted to challenge her rebellious son. Recognizing as she did that she had very little time left before she died, the burden on her heart was for her son Douglas. ' "I may never talk to you again," she continued. "In a short time I am going to be with Jesus. But I want to ask you: Will you meet me there?" '[1]

His mother died within four days and by her graveside it was as if the son could hear his mother's words ringing in his ears: 'Will I meet you in heaven?' He knew that he was travelling on a different road, the one leading to hell, but again he stubbornly hardened his heart against the gospel.

God was at work in his life and he felt increasingly troubled and uneasy with his life and attitude. As a shepherd working on the nearby hills, he found the beauty of creation awesome and slowly accepted the fact that God actually existed and was the Creator. Gradually other questions troubled him. Was this Creator God the one whom his parents knew and trusted? Was there a heaven and hell? What if all he had been taught about the Bible was true?

One night a young lady informed him about an excellent young preacher in the local church. 'You must go and hear him,' she said. A little later he heard the young minister preach and was impressed, as well as disturbed, by his exposition of Revelation 3:17-18.

About three weeks later he met the minister on the road and a long spiritual conversation ensued. All his doubts and fears were dispelled as he understood the way of salvation. 'If I can really have Christ as my Saviour, I'll take him,' Douglas MacMillan commented eventually, and he trusted in the Lord Jesus Christ. He was now on the road to heaven.

The details of conversion vary from Christian to Christian.

Circumstances and backgrounds vary as well as opportunities
for hearing the Bible preached. Some come to faith at an early
age, while others struggle over many years before coming to
faith in Christ. Sadly, some people never come to Christ at all.
What about yourself? Do you, like Douglas MacMillan, have
godly parents and friends, but resist their testimony? A relative might be able to ask you the same question: 'Will I meet
you in heaven?' Why not give priority to this matter and ensure that you are right with God? The Lord will welcome you;
go to the Lord just as you are and he will welcome you.

In 1991 Douglas MacMillan was taken ill suddenly and died,
thus depriving his family and church of a godly man, a powerful preacher and a caring ministry. But he is in heaven with the
Lord — and his parents. And it was all because of Christ and
his glorious sacrifice for sinners. I conclude this brief chapter
with words which arrested my attention when I first read them:

    A person may go to heaven
        Without health,
        Without wealth,
        Without fame,
        Without a great name,
        Without learning,
        Without a job,
        Without culture,
        Without beauty,
        Without friends,
        Without 10,000 other things.
    But he can
        Never go to heaven
        Without Christ.[2]

Appendix I
Heaven: the New Testament data

The term 'heaven' occurs about 244 times in the New Testament, while the adjective 'heavenly' is used twenty-three times. The following details may interest you.

1. In Titus, Philemon and Jude the terms 'heaven' and 'heavenly' are not used at all.

2. In Galatians, 2 Thessalonians and 1 John 'heaven' is only referred to once in each letter; even Romans, 1 Corinthians, Philippians, 1 Thessalonians and James only refer to heaven twice each.

3. The two books with the greater use of the word 'heaven' are the first and last books in the New Testament; in Matthew it occurs seventy-one times and in Revelation fifty-two times.

4. Out of the seventy-one times the word 'heaven' is used in Matthew's Gospel, in thirty-four cases it is used in the phrase 'kingdom of heaven'. If Matthew's thirty-four references to the 'kingdom of heaven' are omitted, then the word 'heaven' occurs more frequently in Revelation than in any other consecutive twenty-two chapters in the Bible.

5. Concerning Matthew's use of the word 'heaven', notice that:

   a. Almost all the references are from the lips of the Lord Jesus Christ.

b. Thirty-three out of the thirty-four references to the 'kingdom of heaven' are spoken by the Lord Jesus, the remaining one (in 3:2) by John the Baptist.

c. The phrase 'from heaven' occurs four times (3:17; 16:1; 21:25; 28:2). Only on one of these occasions was the phrase used by the Lord Jesus.

d. The phrase 'in heaven' is used twenty-one times by Matthew.

A breakdown of these references indicates that:

eleven refer to the 'Father in heaven';
one clearly refers to 'reward in heaven' (5:12);
another is related and eschatological (22:30);
of the other eight references, two refer to our responsibility as Christians to gain 'treasures in heaven'.

6. Heaven is mentioned in:
Mark — nine times;
Luke — thirty-one times;
John — sixteen times;
Acts — twenty-five times.

7. While Mark has the distinction among the four Gospel writers of making the fewest references to heaven, his use of the word is interesting:

three references are eschatological and in the context of the Lord's personal return in glory;
two references are in the context of the Lord's baptism;
one reference relates to his ascension.

8. Within the Gospels, Luke is second only to Matthew for the number of times he uses the word 'heaven' — thirty-one times.

From these references by Luke, the Lord Jesus uses the word 'heaven' in the majority of cases (nineteen times).

In six other references, it is the Lord Jesus who is referred to, in his baptism (twice), birth, Gethsemane, ascension, as well as at prayer.

Like Matthew and Mark, Luke is Christo-centric in his use of the word 'heaven'.

9. In John's Gospel there are sixteen references to 'heaven' and one reference to 'heavenly'.

Eight of these references to 'heaven' are found in 6:31-58; this is the discourse with the Jews in which our Lord refers to himself as the 'bread from heaven'.

Of the remaining eight references, six again are from the mouth of the Lord Jesus (three of which occur in just one verse, 3:13) and the other references concern the Lord's attitude in praying (17:1) and John's testimony regarding his baptism (1:32).

10. Acts uses the word 'heaven' twenty-five times but 'heavenly' only once (26:19).

An analysis of these twenty-five references is again interesting and highlights a particular reason Luke had in writing the Acts. There is considerable discussion at present within New Testament studies concerning the structure and purpose of Acts. A strong apologetic and evangelistic as well as didactic purpose is evident in Acts, in which the success of the gospel and the growth of the church, together with its conflict with the Roman state and Jewish religious authorities, are outlined and illustrated. For these reasons, Acts is distinctive in its use of the term 'heaven' and largely reflects the missionary and cross-cultural work of the church in taking the gospel beyond Samaria 'to the ends of the earth' (Acts 1:8).

Observe the following details about the use of the term 'heaven' in Acts:

a. Of the twenty-five uses of the word 'heaven', at least six times the word is used with reference to God.

These six references emphasize God as Creator, Provider and Ruler. For example, see 4:24: 'Sovereign Lord ... you made the heaven and the earth and the sea, and everything in them' (cf. 7:49; 14:15,17; 17:24). While the Christological perspective is present, it is the glory of the Creator-Ruler God which is emphasized here.

b. 'Heaven' is also used with regard to Christ's ascension (twice in 1:11), Stephen's martyrdom (7:55-56), Saul's conversion (9:3; 22:6; 26:13), Pentecost (2:2,19) and the universality and uniqueness of the Lord Jesus Christ as Saviour (4:12; cf. 2:5).

11. Other New Testament books which I have not mentioned already and which refer to heaven are:

2 Corinthians — three references;
Ephesians — three references;
Colossians — five references;
Hebrews — nine references;
1 Peter — three references;
2 Peter — four references.

12. A major New Testament book on heaven is Revelation. In the four Gospels, references to heaven are not usually accompanied by any description. The purpose of Revelation is distinctive; John the apostle is commanded by the Lord to write those things which he had been privileged to see and hear when given various visions of Christ, the future and heaven (see, for example, 1:1-3,19-20).

13. While the word 'heavenly' occurs twenty-three times in the New Testament, the majority of references are found in Matthew, Ephesians and Hebrews.

Appendix II
Heaven: are there rewards for Christians?

Heaven is a gift; yes, a free gift, purchased by Christ and given freely to all who believe on Jesus Christ. This is the clear, resounding message of the Bible: 'The gift of God is eternal life in Christ Jesus our Lord' (Rom. 6:23; Eph. 2:8-9). No one deserves heaven; it really is God's gift to each Christian. It is all the more surprising, therefore, to be told that God rewards Christians *in* heaven. Is this true? And, if so, on what basis does God reward his people? In order to discuss these matters, I intend to begin by asking four related questions.

I. Four important questions

1. Are Christians rewarded in heaven?

Many writers and theologians think so and here are just a few statements from them:

Louis Berkhof: 'It is also evident from Scripture that there will be degrees in the bliss of heaven.'[1]

Maurice Roberts: 'There will be a reward made to each saint...'[2]

K. Scott Oliphint and Sinclair B. Ferguson: 'Each one of us will be judged by God ... this includes himself and his fellow believers — all Christians will be judged.'[3]

Herbert Lockyer: 'Are some of the saints to have different and higher positions than others?... Scripture expressly declares rewards in the hereafter...'[4]

D. L. Moody: 'If you want to be popular in heaven and get a reward that shall last for ever, you will have to be unpopular here.'[5]

Paul Helm: 'There will be differences in heaven. The heavenly citizens are not clones, nor the product of a celestial assembly-line. They are individuals who retain their individuality. And some will enjoy a different status in heaven from others.'[6]

Bruce Milne: 'Christians also will face a judgement (2 Cor. 5:10)... Two important New Testament passages speak of believers receiving rewards in the afterlife' (1 Cor. 3:10-15; Luke 19:11-26).[7]

Jonathan Edwards: 'We ought to seek high degrees of glory in heaven.'[8]

Wayne Grudem: 'Scripture also teaches that there will be degrees of reward for believers...'[9]

R. T. Kendall: 'Not all who go to heaven will receive a reward at the Judgement Seat of Christ. But all can... All who are saved *are* going to go to heaven but not all who go to heaven will receive a reward.'[10]

H. Z. Cleveland: 'It is possible to be busy in the Lord's service and receive no rewards at all (1 Cor. 3:15; 9:27) or to receive little when one should receive much (2 John 8).'[11]

2. Which Bible references are used in support of degrees of rewards in heaven for Christians?

Gospels

Matt. 5:10-12; 10:41-42; 19:28-29; 20:1-16; 24:45-51; 25:14-30,31-46;
Luke 12:41-47; 19:11-27

Epistles

1 Cor. 3:8,10-15; 9:27;
2 Cor. 5:10.

These are the main New Testament references which we will consider in more detail later.

3. On what basis are rewards given to Christians in heaven?

Most writers rightly emphasize the context of grace in which rewards are given in heaven. Paul Helm, for example, insists that 'Whatever the position turns out to be about rewards in heaven, the dominant fact is the fact of salvation through divine grace, of mercy enjoyed on account of what another has suffered and done.'[12] He adds, 'On the one hand the whole basis of heaven is free, unmerited grace. On the other hand there are differences, and these differences are described as rewards.'[13]

But when we ask these various writers on what basis, or for what reasons, rewards are given in grace to Christians in heaven, the answers vary considerably and, on occasions, disturbingly.

Maurice Roberts explains that a reward will be made to each Christian 'for loving and faithful service to Christ while on earth. The Lord will repay everyone "according as his work shall be" (Revelation 22:12).'[14] The answer is somewhat vague but Roberts suggests it is the quality of our discipleship to Christ which is assessed, a discipleship expressed practically, involving 'earthly losses and crosses', 'sacrifices made here below' and 'every evil suffered for His sake'.[15]

Bruce Milne provides a similar explanation. 'Our judgement,' he writes, 'will be in respect of our stewardship of the gifts, talents, opportunities and responsibilities given in this life. It will be a fatherly judgement...'[16] The nature of stewardship is illustrated differently by Milne but the reference to 'responsibilities' is ambiguous and its extent is not indicated. What is clear is that it is stewardship, rather than sins or progress in sanctification, which is scrutinized and rewarded in final judgement. The reference to 'fatherly judgement' is also reassuring in that it occurs within the context of a secure, loving relationship of grace; in other words, the salvation of the believer is not in doubt.

Louis Berkhof offers a brief but slightly different emphasis: 'Our good works will be the measure of our gracious reward, though they do not merit it.'[17] There are many questions raised by this statement. For example, is the term 'good works' used more widely than stewardship to include the whole area of sanctification? Are the 'good works' judged in terms only of their evidential value in expressing the reality of our justification?

Paul Helm refers to 'ministerial faithfulness and success'[18] in 1 Corinthians 3:12-15 as one important aspect for judgement. More generally, Professor Helm thinks that rewards will be 'given in strict justice in accordance with inner motives and outward actions of the believer'.[19] The rewards of heaven, he stresses, are consistent with 'those degrees of obedient, loving faithfulness in the saints while upon the earth' which are the result of God's grace. As I intend to show later, Helm has a strong case when he relates the 1 Corinthians 3:12-15 passage to ministerial faithfulness. His more general point that 'inner motives and outward actions' are rewarded places the judgement and rewards of believers in a strong, almost exclusive, sanctification, rather than stewardship, context. But how does this relate to justification and the fact that the sins of believers are remembered no more?

Wayne Grudem asks the questions: 'Will all the secret words and deeds of believers, and all their sins, also be revealed' in the judgement and rewarded?[20] 'It seems that this is so,' he answers and uses 1 Corinthians 4:5 in support of his answer.

Herbert Lockyer draws attention to 'the many references to rewards' in the New Testament, all emphasizing the fact that 'It matters very much how we live and labour here…'[21] It is the *'quality'* of our work that matters to God, not its quantity.[22]

H. Z. Cleveland is even more specific and helpful in identifying in the New Testament 'various types of service' which 'merit rewards': enduring testings (James 1:12), diligently seeking God (Heb. 11:6), dying for Christ (Rev. 2:10), faithful pastoral work (1 Peter 5:2-4), faithfully doing God's will and loving his appearing (2 Tim. 4:8), soul-winning (1 Thess. 2:19-20), faithful stewardship (1 Cor. 4:1-5), acts of kindness (Gal. 6:9-10) and hospitality (Matt. 10:40-42).[23]

R. T. Kendall is 'sure of this' fact: 'We who are saved will also be judged; not merely on the basis of whether we are saved or lost but on the basis of our lives as Christians.'[24] Nor is Kendall slow in explaining what this involves. At the judgement seat of Christ, there will be a 'review of my life as a believer',[25] involving especially 'unconfessed sin and ... quiet obedience'.[26] This goes beyond the traditional position held by many evangelicals and I will assess it later in the light of the New Testament references.

4. What is the nature of these rewards in heaven?

Many writers agree with R. T. Kendall on the fact that they do not know precisely what kind of rewards they will receive as Christians in heaven[27] except that they are described in terms of 'reward, praise and crown'.

Milne suggests that faithful stewardship will 'receive an appropriate "reward" in terms of the satisfaction of seeing our work preserved for the eternal kingdom, and perhaps also in terms of additional degrees of responsibility in the heavenly age'.[28] This cautious approach is appropriate in view of the Scripture's relative silence on the subject.

Despite Kendall's earlier acknowledgement of ignorance concerning the rewards, he proceeds from 1 Corinthians 3:14 to tell us about three things which 'make up the reward: ratification, recognition, realization'.[29] The first confirms what we were on earth, the second when all 'recognize the surviving superstructure after the fire of that Day', while 'Realization is when each of us knows exactly what God thinks.'

Millard Erickson admits honestly his tendency at this point to speculate but asks, 'May it not be that the difference in the rewards lies not in the external or objective circumstances, but in the subjective awareness or appreciation of those circumstances?'[30]

II. Rewards in heaven: some key words

So far we have attempted to illustrate the opinions of other Christians concerning rewards in heaven. I hope the exercise has been helpful in clarifying the four related questions but it is now time to ascertain, as far as is possible, what the Bible actually teaches on this subject.

Our immediate task is to begin to examine responsibly the Bible references concerning the subject. We shall do so by looking at some key Bible words: 'reward' or 'wage', 'crown' and 'greatest and least'.

1. Reward or wage

The important Greek word here is *misthos,* which is used in four
related but distinct ways in the New Testament:

> *a.* Wages given to workers. The word is used six times in this
> way — e.g. Matt. 20:8.
> *b.* Wages or reward for wicked behaviour — Acts 1:18; 2 Peter
> 2:13.
> *c.* The general sense of reward, as in John 4:36; 1 Cor. 9:18.
> *d.* Divine rewards. This is the most important use of the word
> and the one which is relevant to our study in this section.

Analysis of passages which use this word

It will be helpful to examine the way in which the Greek word *misthos*
is used in Matthew's Gospel with regard to divine rewards.

Matthew 6:1. 'You will have no *reward* from your Father in heaven.'
This negative statement is emphatic; one reason why they do not
receive a reward from God the Father is that they have received
their coveted reward of praise and admiration from people.

Matthew 6:2,5,16. In these three verses the same statement is used:
'They have received their reward in full.' Leon Morris reminds us
that the verb translated as 'have' in this statement is 'used as a
technical term in commerce with the meaning "receive a sum in *full*
and give a receipt for it" '.[31] The people referred to in these verses
cannot, therefore, 'expect a heavenly reward in addition, for they
have already been "paid in full" '.[32]

A different word, in fact a verb meaning 'to recompense', is used in
Matthew 6:4,6,18: 'Then your Father, who sees what is done in
secret, will reward you.' We are not informed what this reward is.
Quoting Plummer, Leon Morris refers to possible results such as a
good conscience, progress in holy living and knowing God better.[33]
There can be rewards here and now for Christians. While Hendriksen
claims that the reward is given 'on the judgement day'[34] yet he asks,
'And are there not anticipatory rewards even now, such as a good
conscience and rejoicing along with the recipients?'[35]

Matthew 10:41 speaks of 'a prophet's reward' and 'a righteous man's reward'. Reassuringly, the Lord declares that if a person gives the smallest of gifts, such as a cup of cold water, to an insignificant believer, then 'He will certainly not lose his reward' (v. 42).The Greek word *misthos* is used here again and the words used are emphatic. But what is this reward? No details are given although Hendriksen suggests that it includes 'peace of mind now ... public acknowledgement by Christ himself at his return ... and ever afterward all the blessings that are bestowed solely by grace, according to works'.[36]

Summary

From this brief study, two facts emerge. Firstly, the 'reward' given by the Father to believers can be given, at least partly, in this present world. Secondly, the 'reward' can be understood predominantly in terms of eternal life rather than additional rewards given in heaven.

Our Lord's statement in Matthew 5:12, where *misthos* is again used, illustrates the point for us: 'Rejoice and be glad, because great is your reward in heaven, for in the same way they persecuted the prophets who were before you.' 'Great' indicates that the reward is 'far from meagre'[37] and is located in heaven although we are not given any further details.

Lloyd-Jones offers an explanation for the Bible's reticence to 'tell us much about' the reward. 'It is so glorious and wonderful,' he insists, 'that our human language is of necessity almost bound to detract from its glory.'[38]

But, whatever the explanation, the lack of detail in the Bible concerning reward in heaven should make us extremely cautious in approaching the subject. Are some writers guilty of imposing a 'rewards' theology on statements of Scripture which are deliberately vague?[39]

Further references to rewards in Matthew's Gospel, especially in chapters 19, 20, 24 and 25, will be examined later together with other key New Testament statements.

2. Crown

It is often assumed that heavenly rewards for service are described in the Bible as crowns and we now need to ascertain how reliable and biblical this assumption is. Here we are interested in the Greek word *stephanos* and the way in which it is used in the New Testament.

The word is usually translated as 'crown', but originally it referred to a garland given to the winning athlete, or a crown given to a Roman soldier who was brave and victorious in battle. Sometimes in classical literature the word referred to the crown worn by a king, or a garland given to a person in honour of distinguished service. Whatever the precise circumstance, the word was used as an expression of special honour and praise.

Some references to the word *stephanos* in the New Testament are relevant to our subject and we shall refer briefly to each one.

1 Corinthians 9:25: 'Everyone who competes in the games goes into strict training. They do it to get a crown that will not last; but we do it to get a crown that will last for ever.' The word 'crown' occurs only once in the Greek text here but the contrast is a telling one. An athlete sacrifices and competes in order to obtain a temporary, perishable crown, but the Christian perseveres in grace and exercises discipline to get a crown which will 'last for ever'. This crown, however, may be a reference to the blessings and privileges of heaven, rather than to a special reward for Christians in heaven.

Philippians 4:1: 'Therefore, my brothers, you whom I love and long for, my joy and crown...' Ralph Martin calls this last phrase 'words of endearment'.[40] The meaning is that Paul regards the Philippian Christians as his 'reward' and the evidence of the genuineness and fruitfulness of his preaching ministry. These Christians are 'his adorning wreath'.[41] But this is not even a veiled reference to a special reward in heaven.

1 Thessalonians 2:19: 'For what is our hope, our joy, or the crown in which we will glory in the presence of our Lord Jesus Christ when he comes? Is it not you?' The meaning is similar to that of Philippians 4:1 and one writer can claim justifiably that here Paul is 'almost lyrical in his expressions of esteem for his converts'.[42]

2 Timothy 4:8: 'Now there is in store for me the crown of righteousness, which the Lord, the righteous Judge, will award to me on that day — and not only to me, but also to all who have longed for his appearing.' There are two main ways of interpreting this phrase, 'the crown of righteousness', but I prefer to interpret it in the same way as in a parallel phrase, 'the crown of life', as in James 1:12 and Revelation 2:10. On this basis, 'righteousness' is the crown both in terms of imputed and imparted righteousness. This crown is common to *all* believers; 'not only to me,' adds the apostle, 'but also to all who have longed for his appearing'. The phrase cannot, therefore, be used to support the doctrine of special rewards in heaven for some Christians.

James 1:12: 'Blessed is the man who perseveres under trial, because when he has stood the test, he will receive the crown of life that God has promised to those who love him' (cf. Rev. 2:10). Here the Greek genitive translated as 'of life' is descriptive[43] denoting the crown which 'consists of life'; it is not a prize as in 1 Corinthians 9:25. The reward is identified as 'life' — that is, eternal life and the enjoyment of God throughout eternity.[44] Once again there is no reference here to degrees of rewards in heaven. Rather the 'crown of life' is 'promised to those who love him' and persevere in grace, like all genuine believers, despite severe trials in this world.

1 Peter 5:4: 'And when the Chief Shepherd appears, you will receive the crown of glory that will never fade away.' In the context the apostle Peter is addressing church elders. Such leaders must assume the duties of pastoral oversight in a God-honouring manner and not for purposes of financial gain or power-seeking. By contrast, they must be 'examples to the flock' (v. 3). Their reward at the return of the Lord Jesus will be 'the crown of glory' which probably emphasizes their share in future glory and heavenly life.[45] There does not seem to be a reference in this statement to degrees of rewards in heaven.

Revelation 3:11: 'Hold on to what you have, so that no one will take your crown.' The church in Philadelphia has already obtained the prize of the Lord's approval for its perseverance and victory in trials. Now the church must hold on to this prize by continuing to persevere in faith and obedience. However, Philip Hughes insists there is 'no suggestion here that God's work of grace may fail in the end'.[46] The emphasis is on the need for sincerity and commitment 'as we persevere in the midst of trials and afflictions'.

Summary

None of the foregoing verses in which the word 'crown' is used
provides us with a clear, undisputed reference to degrees of rewards
in heaven. Possibly the verse which comes closest to implying this
doctrine is 1 Peter 5:4, but this is confined to church elders.

3. Greatest and least in the kingdom

Our Lord's teaching on this subject needs to be noted, for it is relevant and challenging. There are three main passages with their respective parallels in the Gospels which concentrate on this theme:

Matthew 18:1-4 (cf. Mark 9:33-37; Luke 9:46-48). It is the disciples here who ask their Lord, 'Who is the greatest in the kingdom
of heaven?' The Lord's answer is patient and gracious in its tone
but uncompromising in its message. True greatness involves humility or 'humble trustfulness',[47] not ruthless ambition and selfishness.
In which ways can a humble person be understood to be 'the greatest' in the kingdom? One way is that such a person pleases God and
receives praise from God, while also, secondly, he reflects the attitude and example of the Lord Jesus, the Servant-King. Another way
is that the person is entrusted by God with important responsibilities and privileges in the church here and now. Verse 4 appears to
emphasize a present fulfilment of kingdom 'greatness' in this life.

Matthew 20:20-28 (cf. Mark 10:35-45). The request is made by the
mother of James and John on behalf of her children. Clearly the
teaching of Matthew 18:1-4 is assumed here, namely, that greatness
must be measured by humility. But the mother wanted a superior
and privileged position for her two sons in the future consummation
of the kingdom. Neither the mother nor her sons understood the
significance of this request (v. 22). The answer by James and John
reveals their loyalty to Jesus but also their self-confidence and pride.
In verse 23 Jesus goes on to predict the martyrdom of James and the
banishment of John to the Isle of Patmos for the sake of the gospel.
They will indeed suffer, but only God the Father decides on positions of glory for believers in the kingdom.

This conversation soon led to an angry exchange of words between the two brothers and the other apostles. It was necessary for the Lord Jesus to intervene. His intervention involved an important elaboration on the nature and uniqueness of greatness within the kingdom of God. By contrast, worldly leaders spend their energies and time in reaching positions of power and then rule as tyrants and oppressors over their subjects (v. 25). 'Not so with you,' the Lord warns, and repeats teaching he had given earlier, in 18:1-4. True greatness, according to Christ, is obtained by self-giving, loving, serving others and modelling one's attitude on the example of Jesus (Matt. 20:28).

Luke 22:24-30. Some of the verses in this section are similar to other statements elsewhere in the Gospels and the contrast between ruthless, worldly leaders and Christians is sustained in verse 25, together with the warning reminiscent of Matthew 20:26: 'But you are not to be like that.'

What is of particular interest to us in this section is the reference to rewards in verses 29 and 30. David Gooding sums up the thrust of these two verses in the following way: 'Their schooling done and loyalty to Christ tested by suffering, they would be rewarded in the age to come with the delight of close personal fellowship with him in his glory and active participation with him in the government (verses 28-30).'[48]

Hendriksen may be justified in interpreting the 'kingdom' (v. 29) as 'royal rule',[49] indicating that the apostles will share in Christ's rule in its final and glorious expression. To 'eat and drink' suggests the joys and intimacies of heavenly fellowship with Christ, whereas to 'sit on thrones' is probably an illustration of 'royal rule'. Whether this involves judging or ruling the 'restored new Israel', or all the elect (Jews and Gentiles), is not clear but 'Those who have been closest to Jesus here will also be closest to him there.'[50]

Summary

While specific rewards in the future state are implied here, it is extremely difficult to decide to what extent these rewards are shared by *all* believers.

III Rewards in heaven: some key biblical statements

Having examined a number of key words in the New Testament, such as 'reward', 'crown', 'greatest' and 'least', we have been able to conclude that there is very little support from these key words for the doctrine of degrees of rewards in heaven. An important exception is Luke 22:28-30, but even here there are serious difficulties in interpreting the verses. We now move forward to consider some key statements which are popularly believed to teach degrees of rewards for Christians in heaven. Once again we need to be fair in our study of these important biblical statements.

Eight key statements, or passages, in the New Testament have been chosen for more detailed attention here: Matthew 19:28-29; 20:1-16; 24:45-51; 25:14-30 with Luke 19:11-27; Matthew 25:31-46; Luke 12:41-47; 1 Corinthians 3:12-15; 2 Corinthians 5:10.

Reasons for selecting these passages

The sampling of these eight passages has been determined by the following considerations:

    a. They are *generally* regarded as teaching degrees of rewards in heaven for Christians.

    b. These eight statements are assumed to be *clear* in their support of the doctrine of rewards.

    c. Such statements, and especially those from 1 Corinthians 3 and 2 Corinthians 5, have been highlighted in contemporary writing and with somewhat dubious conclusions. As I hope you can see, the choice of these eight statements is by no means arbitrary and now we must consider them in turn.

Key statements from the Gospels

Matthew 19:28-29 — The Lord's reply to Peter

'We have left everything to follow you!' declared Peter. 'What then will there be for us?' In other words, he wanted to know whether they would be rewarded for their sacrifice. The Lord's answer in verse 28 is similar, though not identical, to the words of Luke 22:30 which we considered earlier. The words in Matthew's account refer to the future return of Christ in glory and the cosmic renewal when the apostles will rule with Christ. In verse 29 the Lord then refers to all Christians who have sacrificed for the sake of Christ; they 'will receive a hundred times as much and will inherit eternal life'.

Leon Morris believes that the 'hundred times as much' really 'points to uncountable blessings'.[51] William Hendriksen justifiably suggests that this hundredfold reward will be enjoyed by Christians 'even in the present day and age and before death'.[52] Hendriksen adds that they 'even enjoy their material possessions ... far more than the ungodly enjoy theirs'[53] in this world; on the 'new earth' also the 'material blessings will be added to the spiritual'. Donald A. Hagner emphasizes, however, that 'The greatest blessing of all will be the inheritance of eternal life.'[54]

We may therefore conclude that Christians receive a hundred-fold reward, partly if not largely, in this world, because of their sacrifices for Christ before enjoying eternal life in all its fulness after death. This statement by the Lord Jesus, therefore, does not provide strong support for the doctrine of degrees of rewards in heaven for Christians.

Matthew 20:1-16 — The parable of the workers in the vineyard

'The point of the parable,' writes R. T. Kendall, 'is to demonstrate that it is God's sovereign prerogative to do as He pleases with each of us.'[55] Yes, God's sovereignty is emphasized, but it is divine sovereignty in dispensing grace and mercy to needy sinners which stands out in the parable. The action of the vineyard owner points to the kindness, generosity, pity and grace of God, so that the 'Jews have no precedence over the Gentiles nor the man saved young over the one saved when old'.[56] Here is the 'gospel of the penitent thief' with the 'focus on grace shown to those enlisted in the eleventh hour, and regarded by others as not worth hiring'.[57]

While this parable may not have been given to refute the idea of rewards, yet the parable offers no support for the traditional doctrine of degrees of rewards in heaven. Craig L. Blomberg observes that most expositors agree that 'Jesus is teaching about a fundamental equality here among those who are truly his disciples. All are rewarded alike.'[58]

Matthew 24:45-51 — The parable of the faithful and wise servant

Leon Morris is in no doubt that it is the distinction between unbe-
lievers/hypocrites and believers which is underlined in this parable,
not a distinction between believers.[59] The 'then' in verse 45 estab-
lishes a link with the preceding section where vigilance and watch-
fulness are urged upon believers in the light of Christ's sudden, unexpected return. Faithfulness is now urged in addition in this parable, as a necessary characteristic of true believers. A faithful servant will be ready for the coming of the Son of Man by living an
obedient, Christ-honouring life.[60]

We may therefore conclude that this parable does not support the
doctrine of degrees of rewards in heaven.

Matthew 25:14-30; Luke 19:11-27 — The parable of the talents

There are obvious similarities as well as differences between these
two accounts. In both, the distinguished owner and lord entrusted
money to each servant before undertaking a long journey. On his
return, he required these servants to explain what they had achieved
with his money. In each parable the first two servants were praised
and rewarded for their diligence, while the last servant was rebuked
and, in Matthew's account, punished.

But the main differences between these two stories also need to
be noted. In Matthew, the monies allocated are large but variable,
whereas in Luke the amounts are small and identical for each servant. For Matthew the punishment for the 'worthless servant' is severe, while in Luke the servant is deprived of his money but not
himself punished.

It is possible that the Lord Jesus adapted this one theme on two
distinct occasions.[61] Bruce Milne sees Luke 19:11-27 and 1 Corinthians 3:10-15 as together forming 'two important NT passages'
which 'speak of believers receiving rewards in the afterlife'.[62] Milne,
however, warns us that 'Luke 19:11-26 must be interpreted with
care, since parables in general are presented to make one central
point and we must not press the secondary details.'[63] This is a necessary warning and Hendriksen tells us what he considers to be the
'one central point' in Luke's account. 'As to the parable's ultimate
meaning,' he writes, 'the reference is to what will happen to Christ-
rejecters when he returns.'[64] While David Gooding claims that Luke's

parable teaches 'a number of exceedingly important principles', one such principle is that the Lord is here seeking to 'represent a false servant exposed at last as an unbeliever'.[65]

Both parables basically distinguish between true and false believers; they are not primarily informing us about differences between believers. In Matthew's account, for example, the first two servants are completely faithful and, despite being given different amounts of money, are treated identically afterwards by their master (vv. 21,23). In Luke's account, each servant is given the same amount of money and the first two manage to make a hundred or fifty per cent profit respectively. But how should we interpret their success? Both were equally faithful and received the same commendation in verses 17 and 19. Was the difference in achievement due to different abilities and gifts rather than degrees of faithfulness? This seems a reasonable interpretation in the light of the context.

Some will still want to press these parables in support of degrees of rewards in heaven. Well, even if these two accounts are accepted as distinguishing between believers in heaven, such distinctions only reflect and continue the different gifts and abilities with which believers are endowed in this life. It is interesting to observe that the distinctions are not introduced or changed in any way at the final judgement.

Matthew 25:31-46 — The sheep and the goats

Many writers agree that this is not a parable; it is 'a poetic description' of the fulfilment of the prophecy in 16:27.[66] It is 'a very dramatic, frequently symbolic, description of the last judgement'[67] or 'a picture of the Last Judgement, an eschatological vision'.[68] Again, what comes to the fore here is the fundamental difference between believers and unbelievers. The contrast is seen clearly when verses 34 and 41 are compared as well as their ultimate fate underlined in verse 46.

These verses in 25:31-46 provide no support at all for the teaching of different degrees of rewards in heaven.

Luke 12:41-44 — The faithful and wise servant

From Luke 12:35 through to 13:21 the 'kingdom-spirit' motif gives way to the dominant note of judgement. In the immediate context of chapter 12 the theme of material possessions is now placed in verses 35-47 within the perspective of the Lord's return in glory. When he returns, all his servants will be responsible to him for the way in which they have handled their material possessions as well as their gifts and abilities. What is apparent in this parable is a very strong emphasis on the unfaithful servant. Whereas only three short opening verses are devoted to the faithful servant (vv. 42-44), a much more detailed description is given of the unfaithful servant in two long verses (vv. 45-46). In fact, the application in verses 47-48 relates primarily, if not exclusively, to the unfaithful servant's punishment, which is moderated depending on the degree of knowledge concerning the master's will. 'Let a man profess what he will,' insists David Gooding, 'if he constantly and consistently behaves in an unchristian way, he is not a true believer and the Second Coming will expose him for what he is.'[69]

Two questions remain to be asked. Firstly, does verse 42 have in mind the church pastor or officers who are responsible for feeding and caring for believers under their pastoral charge?[70] Secondly, are degrees of rewards in heaven taught in this parable? While most commentators[71] reply positively to the second question, I tend to give a negative answer. Responsibility and accountability are most certainly stressed, but are these principles illustrated primarily to highlight the enormous differences between believers and unbelievers?

IV. Two crucial texts from the epistles

We have almost concluded this detailed and rather long study of rewards in heaven. We first referred to the different ways in which some Christians have answered important questions relating to the subject. Next we began to look at relevant key words in the New Testament and concluded that terms like 'reward', 'crown' and 'greatest and least' do not support the traditional teaching of rewards. Our third section was devoted to an examination of key statements in the Gospels of Matthew and Luke. We concluded that there appear to be special rewards for some (Matt. 19:28), while it is unlikely that Luke 19:11-27 refers to degrees of rewards in heaven for believers generally. To put it more briefly, the evidence for the teaching of different rewards in heaven is not as firmly grounded in the New Testament as many Christians have supposed.

Two crucial texts remain to be considered, namely, 1 Corinthians 3:8,10-15 and 2 Corinthians 5:10. There can be no doubt at all that these two texts are crucial to our study.

One reason for their importance is that they are frequently used to support, and even 'prove', the teaching of different rewards in heaven. In fact, these are the two main texts employed to support the teaching of degrees of rewards. And the evidence of these two texts is assumed to be clear and indisputable. Furthermore, several writers and commentators already referred to tend to interpret other New Testament statements, especially in the Gospels, in the light of these two key texts.

But there is another reason why we must attach considerable importance to these texts and consider them in detail here. Several contemporary writers on the subject believe that these texts support the doctrine of rewards. Interestingly, R. T. Kendall has written two books in which he makes extensive use and application of these two texts from 1 and 2 Corinthians.[72] Paradoxically, these two books have attracted both widespread criticism and also applause; they are well written, cogently argued and helpfully illustrated. It is not my intention to review or even reply in detail here to these books, but I will challenge as graciously as possible my friend's interpretation and application of these two crucial texts.

1 Corinthians 3:8-15

'Few passages of the New Testament,' warns Carson, 'have been abused by preachers and writers more than this one.'[73] And it is a necessary warning, for 1 Corinthians 3 has been used to support the unbiblical theory of purgatory as well as the division of mankind into three major groups, namely, unbelievers, spiritual and also carnal believers. That is not all. This chapter is a major text for those who claim there are degrees of rewards in heaven for Christians. For example, in his book *When God says 'Well done!'*, R. T. Kendall devotes thirteen of the nineteen chapters to an exposition and application of 1 Corinthians 3:9-15. According to Kendall, the chapter 'gives us more details of what Paul calls the "judgement seat of Christ" in 2 Corinthians 5:10'.[74] It is now time for us to examine this section of 1 Corinthians 3 in more detail.

1. The context

From 1 Corinthians 1:10 to 4:21 there is one major concern for the apostle, and this relates to the disunity and cliques within the Corinthian church. Lying behind these divisions were 'two deeper problems',[75] namely, the undermining of the significance and centrality of the cross of Christ and also a wrong attitude towards Christian ministers. In chapters 3 and 4 Paul spends a lot of time 'clearing up these misapprehensions'[76] and he does so by stressing three points:

a. In 3:1-4 those who foster divisions give evidence of their spiritual immaturity.

b. In 3:5-17 such people misunderstand Christian leadership for two reasons:

Firstly, men like Paul and Apollos are only the Lord's servants; it is God who blesses and prospers their work (vv. 5-9);

Secondly, God builds his church and cares for it; therefore, church leaders are accountable to God for the way in which they work within the church (vv. 10-15).

c. In 3:16-17 the church is God's temple and the Lord jealously protects it as the place where the Holy Spirit resides. Both preachers and members of the church, therefore, need to be careful how they build and behave within such a church.

2. Who are the builders — ministers only or all Christians?

Who are the builders referred to in verses 10,12,14,15? Charles Hodge is emphatic: 'In the whole context he is speaking of ministers and therefore this clause [at the end of verse 10] must be considered as a warning addressed to them.'[77] Carson agrees, observing that the end of verse 9 is 'transitional'[78] and moves from a farming (vv. 6-9) to a building (vv. 9-15) illustration. A contrast is made between Christians and church leaders; the former are 'God's field, God's building' whereas the latter are the builders. And such leaders are accountable to God for the quality of their ministries.

At this point, Kendall acknowledges the distinction between 'we' and 'you' in verses 5-9,[79] but insists that all Christians, as well as leaders, are accountable to, and judged by, the Lord, thus receiving different degrees of reward in heaven. Christians are responsible to God, claims Kendall, for their 'application of teaching', their 'approach to temptation', their 'attitude toward trial' and their 'ability with the tongue'.[80] According to Kendall, if the quality of our lives and work as Christians is not satisfactory then we shall 'suffer loss' (v. 15), that is, lose our rewards in heaven, although saved.[81]

But I want to challenge this interpretation by asking four related questions.

Firstly, *what is the 'wood, hay or straw' referred to in verse 12?* For Kendall, it refers mainly to 'undiscovered sin', 'unconfessed sin' and 'unrestituted sin'.[82] However, notice that at the end of verse 10 the apostle is still talking about 'the exclusive power, wisdom and authority bound up with the gospel'.[83] This is confirmed in verse 11, where the only true foundation of the Christian church is Jesus Christ and him crucified,[84] so that the building being erected is the church which is later described in verse 16 as 'God's temple'. The 'wood, hay or straw', therefore, refers to the quality of the work done by preachers and church leaders in building God's church. 'The whole discussion,' Hodge emphasizes, 'has reference to preachers and their duties.'[85]

This becomes clearer by asking a further question: *what is meant by 'work' in verse 13?* Again, Kendall understands the term as 'the sum total of our spiritual progress',[86] but this interpretation is unjustified in the immediate context for 'work' is synonymous with that of 'building' in verses 10, 12 and 14. Both terms refer to the crucial task of preaching and applying the Word in the church.

Thirdly, *what is meant by 'loss' in verse 15?* Paul is not suggesting that some Christians can be lost and fail to reach heaven. Not at all, and verse 15 confirms the fact. Nor is Paul implying that though a Christian reaches heaven yet he can lose a reward there. Rather he is referring to church leaders who are guilty of 'shoddy workmanship' and using 'inferior materials';[87] they mix truth with error, suppress the message of the cross and employ methods as well as standards which are superficial and worldly. This may well include people who claim to become Christians within a church context but are not really converted. Their work as preachers will not stand God's scrutiny in the final day and it has no permanent value.

What does the term 'reward' refer to, then? It appears to include rejoicing on the part of ministers over those who have become Christians under their ministries and matured in the faith (1 Thess.

2:19). In addition, it includes praise from God for the quality and faithfulness of their ministries. However, such a reward as divine praise or rejoicing in fruitful ministries does not entail degrees of rewards. Nor is it clear what the implied object of 'he will suffer loss' is in verse 15. Many assume that it is 'his reward' in verse 14. However, there is another noun, namely, 'the work' in the early part of verse 14 (the NIV translates as 'what he has built') which links even better with the 'loss' mentioned early in verse 15. If so, the 'reward' becomes 'nothing more or less than knowing that they did spend substantial time on building things that would last into eternity: winning people to the Lord, disciplining them, being good stewards of all the resources with which God entrusted them and the like'.[88]

2 Corinthians 5:10

As Craig Blomberg observes, most commentators accept that this text 'refers back' to 1 Corinthians 3, so 'What one does with the former text must carry over to the latter. And both of these texts speak only of judgement day, not of an everlasting hierarchy in heaven.'[89]

While the apostle Paul is speaking of his apostolic ministry from 2 Corinthians 2:12 to at least 6:10 or 7:16, it is clear in 5:10 that all Christians will appear before Christ. The Greek text makes abundantly clear what the purpose of this judgement is: 'that each one may receive what is due to him for the things done while in the body, whether good or bad'.

At this point R. T. Kendall claims that 'We are going to have to give an account of how we have lived as Christians...'[90] This is what Kendall calls 'that ultimate test'[91] and 'the fiery trial above'[92] when our spiritual progress will be publicly and finally assessed, and then rewarded by Christ.[93] For some, it will be 'the most extreme form of chastening',[94] a most terrible event' which involves 'two major things', namely: 'seeing God's own grievance with us and having others see it as well'.[95] Our salvation is not in jeopardy, adds Kendall,[96] but 'undiscovered sin',[97] ;unconfessed sin'[98] and 'unrestituted sin'[99] will be exposed by the Lord. Kendall's challenge is: 'Deal with it now, and it will not show up then. Sweep it under the carpet now, and it will come out then.' In other words,

2 Corinthians 5:10 for Kendall refers to sanctification rather than justification, to our 'stake' as Christians rather than to our 'standing' in Christ before God[100] and involves the exposure of all sins we have not previously dealt with.

But is this correct? Is that what the apostle teaches in this text? By way of reply and assessment, consider the following two arguments.

Firstly, the Greek word translated 'receive' points to the whole pattern of the Christian's behaviour rather than to individual actions, sins and omissions as Kendall claims. This word is in the aorist tense and, as Ralph Martin observes, Paul's use of the word 'suggests a constative force'.[101] What this means is that the action is conceived as a whole 'without reference to the beginning, progress or end'.[102] This means that the Christian's behaviour 'is viewed by Christ as a unity, not as a concatenation of individual acts'.[103] There is a strong suggestion, therefore, that in 2 Corinthians 5:10 the apostle Paul has in view the ultimate vindication of Christians and the difference between believers and unbelievers.

Secondly, this interpretation is confirmed by the fact that the statement at the end of verse 10, namely, 'whether good or bad' is 'constructed with a change to the singular neuter'.[104] The significance of this is that while each individual is judged in the light of his or her behaviour, it is not the individual's detailed actions which are judged, but rather the pattern and direction of his behaviour. A. Plummer also confirms that 'The change to the neuter singular is significant ... conduct in each case will be judged as a whole... It is character rather than separate acts that will be rewarded or punished ... it is what he did during his lifetime that is summed up and estimated as a total.'[105] In other words, it highlights the enormous difference between believers and unbelievers rather than degrees of rewards in heaven for believers.

Conclusion

These two key texts in 1 Corinthians 3 and 2 Corinthians 5:10 speak clearly of judgement but they do *not* teach 'an everlasting hierarchy in heaven'[106] for Christians. To put it in another way, Christians will not be distinguished from each other in heaven on the ground of their lives and works as believers.[107]

Notes

Chapter 1 — Heaven: a shock!
1. Published by Banner of Truth Trust, 1959. See, for example, p.737.
2. Donald Guthrie, *New Testament Theology,* IVP, 1981, p.874.

Chapter 2 — Heaven on earth?
1. *Letters of Samuel Rutherford,* Banner of Truth, 1973, p.105.
2. Thomas Brooks, *Heaven on Earth,* Banner of Truth edition, Puritan Paperbacks, 1961, pp.14-15.
3. Charles Spurgeon, *Metropolitan Tabernacle Pulpit,* vol. 37/1891, Banner of Truth, 1970, p.538.
4. Quoted by John Gerstner in *Jonathan Edwards on Heaven and Hell,* Baker Book House, 1980, p.9.
5. Spurgeon, *Metropolitan Tabernacle Pulpit,* vol. 37, p.537.

Chapter 3 — A fleeting shadow
1. Quoted by W. Barrett in *Irrational Man,* Mercury, London, 1964.
2. Augustine, *Confessions,* Oxford University Press, 1991, 1. i. 1, p.3.
3. C. S. Lewis, 'The weight of glory' in *Screwtape Proposes a Toast,* Collins, 1965, pp.97-8.

Chapter 4 — Death and all that
1. Quoted by Eberhard Jüngel in *Death: The Riddle and the Mystery,* Westminster Press, Philadelphia, 1974.
2. Three different words are translated as 'hell' in the Authorized Version of the Bible. The Hebrew word *She'ol* and the Greek *Hades* refer either to the grave or the state of death, but also sometimes to the state of the ungodly in hell. The Greek word *Gehenna* describes the abode and punishment of unbelievers in hell especially after the final judgement.

Chapter 7 — Heaven: what it really means
1. J. I. Packer, *Concise Theology,* IVP, 1993, p.264.
2. See, e.g., Wilbur Smith, *The Biblical Doctrine of Heaven,* Moody Press, 1968. p.28.

3. As above.
4. Millard J. Erickson, *Christian Theology*, quoted by Wayne Grudem in *Systematic Theology: An introduction to biblical doctrine*, IVP, 1994, p.1159.
5. Guthrie, *New Testament Theology*, p.875.
6. As above, p.880.
7. A. A. Hodge, *Outlines of Theology*, Banner of Truth Trust, 1983, p.578.
8. Packer, *Concise Theology*, p.269.
9. Grudem, *Systematic Theology*, p.1159.

Chapter 8 — Heaven: where it is
1. What D. A. Carson calls 'two entirely antithetical realms', see *The Gospel According to John*, IVP, 1991, p.342.
2. B. F. Westcott, *The Gospel according to St John*, 1892, p. 130.
3. For example, see John A. T. Robinson, *Honest to God*, SCM, 1963, p.13.
4. *Concise Oxford Dictionary*, Oxford University Press, 1976, 6th edition.

Chapter 9 — God is present in heaven as well as everywhere
1. Louis Berkhof, *Systematic Theology*, Banner of Truth, 1959, p.60.
2. As above, p.61.
3. It is well worth reading his *Attributes of God* on this point (*Charnock's Works, vol. 1, Existence of God, Practical Atheism*, London, 1815 — quote on p.537, but read pp.526-95).
4. See, for example, Hodge, *Outlines of Theology*, p.141; also R. B. Kuiper, *The Glorious Body of Christ*, Banner of Truth, 1967, pp.339-43; Grudem, *Systematic Theology*, pp.175-7.
5. *The Works of John Owen*, vol. 12, Banner of Truth, 1967, p.90.

Chapter 10 — Heaven and Christ
1. Carson, *The Gospel according to John*, p.139.
2. W. Hendriksen, *The Gospel of John*, Banner of Truth, 1959, p.90.
3. J. C. Ryle, *Expository Thoughts on the Gospels: John*, James Clarke, 1957, vol. i, p.41.
4. J. C. Ryle, *Expository Thoughts on the Gospels: John*, Evangelical Press, 1985, vol. iv, p.220.
5. Carson, *Gospel according to John*, p.301.

Chapter 11 — Heaven: where it will be
1. Packer, *Concise Theology*, p.269.
2. A. A. Hodge, *The Confession of Faith: A handbook of Christian doctrine expounding the Westminster Confession*, Banner of Truth Trust, 1958, p.383. Professor Hodge (1823-1886) spent several years teaching systematic theology in Princeton Seminary.
3. William Hendriksen, *The Bible on the Life Hereafter*, Baker, 1975, p.214.
4. H. Hoeksema, *Reformed Dogmatics*, Reformed Free Publishing Association, Grand Rapids, 1973, p.863.
5. As above, pp.863-4.
6. Grudem, *Systematic Theology*, p.1160.
7. As above, p.1161.

8. As above, p.1162.
9. *Westminster Confession of Faith,* Section I, of Christ the Mediator.
10. *Westminster Confession of Faith,* Section V, of Christ the Mediator.

Chapter 12 — Heaven: an intermediate state

1. A. A. Hoekema, *The Bible and the Future,* Paternoster, 1994, p.274.
2. As above.
3. Grudem, *Systematic Theology,* p.1158.
4. D. Martyn Lloyd-Jones, *Exposition of Romans 8:17-38, The Final Perseverance of the Saints,* Banner of Truth, 1975, pp.71-2.
5. As above, p.86.
6. K. Scott Oliphint and Sinclair B. Ferguson, *Hoping for Heaven: A look beyond this life,* Crossway Book, 1995, p.68.
7. Hoekema, *The Bible and the Future,* pp.276-7.
8. As above, p.277.
9. Oliphint & Ferguson, *Hoping for Heaven,* p.85.
10. Lloyd-Jones, *Romans 8:17-39,* p.54.
11. Hoekema, *The Bible and the Future,* p.278.
12. As above.
13. As above, p.279.
14. Oliphint & Ferguson, *Hoping for Heaven,* p.86.
15. As above, p.87.
16. Hoekema, *The Bible and the Future,* p.283.
17. As above, p.276; see also Lloyd-Jones, *Romans 8:17-39,* p.83.
18. As above, p.78.
19. Simon J. Kistemaker, *Acts,* Baker, 1990, p.136.
20. Hoekema, *The Bible and the Future,* p.282.
21. As above, Also refer to the exposition of this passage by Lloyd-Jones in *Romans 8:17-39* (pp.14-119) which is very clear and challenging.
22. Hoekema, *The Bible and the Future,* p.284.
23. Bernard Ramm, *Them he Glorified,* Eerdmans, 1963, p.106.
24. Oliphint & Ferguson, *Hoping for Heaven,* pp.68-70.
25. As above, p.88.
26. Lloyd-Jones, *Romans 8:17-39,* p.75.
27. Hoekema, *The Bible and the Future,* p.284.
28. Lloyd-Jones, *Romans 8:17-39,* pp.89-90; see also Grudem, *Systematic Theology,* p.1161.
29. Hoekema, *The Bible and the Future,* p.285.
30. Grudem, *Systematic Theology,* p.1158.
31. As above, pp.1163-4.

Chapter 13 — Heaven: an eternal state

1. *The Works of Jonathan Edwards,* vol.2, Banner of Truth, 1974, p.632.
2. As above, p.631.
3. As above, p.630.
4. As above, p.617.
5. D. Martyn Lloyd-Jones, *Studies in the Sermon on the Mount,* vol.1, IVP, 1959, pp.71-2.

6. Charles Hodge, *An Exposition of the First Epistle to the Corinthians,* Banner of Truth, 1958, pp.62-3.
7. *Works of Jonathan Edwards,* p.632.
8. As above.
9. As above, p.620.
10. Hoekema, *The Bible and the Future,* p.276.
11. Charles Hodge, *Commentary on the Epistle to the Romans,* Eerdmans, 1953, p.272.
12. Hendriksen, *The Bible on the Life Hereafter,* p.207.
13. Oliphint & Ferguson, *Hoping for Heaven,* p.87.
14. Lloyd-Jones, *Romans 8:17-39,* p.86.
15. As above, p89.
16. As above, p.88.

Chapter 14 — Heaven: when Christians go there
1. Quoted by J. C. Ryle in *Five English Reformers,* Banner of Truth, 1960, p.134.
2. Paul Helm, *The Last Things,* Banner of Truth, 1989, p.45.
3. Lloyd-Jones, *Romans 8:17-39,* p.88.
4. *Works of John Flavel,* vol. 1, Banner of Truth, 1968, p.401

Chapter 15 — Heaven: does everybody go there?
1. Richard J. Bauckham, *Themelios,* vol. 4:2, January 1979, p.48.
2. See *Lumen Gentium, Vatican Council II,* vol. 1, Costello Publishing Company, 1984, p.16.
3. Leslie Newbigin, *The Finality of Christ,* London, 1969, p.61.
4. Karl Rahner, *Christianity and Non-Christian Religions,* Fount, 1980.
5. Hans Küng, *Christian Revelation and World Religions,* J. Neuner, 1967, p.52.
6. See his *Christianity at the Centre* (1968 & 1977), later published in 1983 as *The Second Christianity;* also his *Evil and the God of Love* (1984), *God and the Universe of Faiths* (1973), *God Has Many Names* (1980).
7. See my *An Angry God?,* Evangelical Press of Wales, 1991, pp.39-69.
8. Clark Pinnock, A *Wideness in God's Mercy,* Zondervan, 1992.
9. John Sanders, *No Other Name,* Eerdmans, 1992.
10. Blurb on back cover of *A Wideness in God's Mercy.*
11. Statement by Gabriel Fackre on back cover of *No Other Name.*
12. Sanders, *No Other Name,* p.246.
13. Hywel Jones, *Only One Way,* Day One Publications, 1996, p.15.
14. As above, p.62.
15. Pinnock, *A Wideness in God's Mercy,* p.107.
16. See Jones, *Only One Way,* pp.60-97.

Chapter 16 — Worth climbing?
1. A. Wainwright, *Fell-Walking with Wainwright: 18 of the author's favourite walks in Lakeland,* Penguin Group, 1984, p.162.
2. As above.
3. As above.
4. A. Wainwright (with photographs by Derry Brabbs), *Wainwright's Favourite Lakeland Mountains,* BCA by arrangement with Michael Joseph Ltd. London, 1991, pp.187, 196.

5. Quoted by Gerstner, *Jonathan Edwards on Heaven and Hell,* p.11.
6. As above, p.12.
7. Derec Llwyd Morgan, *The Great Awakening in Wales,* Epworth Press, 1988, p.251.
8. As above, p.252.

Chapter 17 — Heaven: our home
1. Guthrie, *New Testament Theology,* p.879.
2. See, for example, John 3:14-15; 6:53-56; 10:11-15,18; 12:23-24,27.
3. Carson, *The Gospel according to John,* p.489.
4. Hendriksen, *The Gospel of John,* p.265.
5. R. V. G. Tasker, *The Gospel according to St John: an introduction and commentary,* Tyndale, IVP, 1960, p.171.
6. John Brown, *Discourses and Sayings of our Lord,* Banner of Truth, 1967, vol. 3, p.22.
7. Ryle, *Expository Thoughts on John,* Evangelical Press, p.181.
8. Brown, *Discourses and Sayings of our Lord,* p.22.
9. Quoted by Herbert Lockyer in *The Gospel of the Life Beyond,* Henry E. Walter, 1967, p.23.

Chapter 18 — Heaven: our Father's home
1. This is argued convincingly by Don Carson in *The Gospel according to John,* pp.488-9.
2. See Gerstner, *Jonathan Edwards on Heaven and Hell,* pp.19-23.
3. Tasker, *The Gospel according to St John,* p.171.
4. Carson, *The Gospel according to John,* p.489.
5. Hendriksen, *The Bible on the Life Hereafter,* p.211.

Chapter 19 — Heaven: with the Lord
1. Thomas Boston, *Human nature in its Fourfold State,* Banner of Truth, 1964, p.449.
2. This can be seen by comparing 2 Corinthians 12:2 with 12:4, and Revelation 2:7 with 22:14,19 and 21:1-2.
3. Ryle, *Expository Thoughts on John,* Evangelical Press, p.226.
4. As above, p.227.
5. Hendriksen, *The Gospel of John,* p.366.
6. William Hendriksen, *New Testament Commentary: Philippians,* Banner of Truth, 1962, p.78.
7. Leon Morris, *The Epistles of Paul to the Thessalonians: an introduction and commentary,* Tyndale, IVP, 1956, p.89.

Chapter 20 — Heaven: seeing the Lord
1. Lloyd-Jones, *Studies in the Sermon on the Mount,* vol. i, p.106.
2. Hendriksen, *The Gospel of John,* p.367.
3. Westcott, *The Gospel according to St John,* p.247.
4. Carson, *The Gospel according to John,* p.569.
5. William H. Gould (ed.), *The Works of John Owen,* Banner of Truth, 1965, vol. vii, p.337.
6. I. Kuhn, *In the Arena,* OMF Books, 1988, pp.321-2.

7. John Calvin, *Institutes of the Christian Religion,* James Clarke, 1953, IV.XVII.39.
8. Gerstner, *Jonathan Edwards on Heaven and Hell,* p.47.
9. As above, p.45.
10. W. G. T. Shedd, *Sermons to the Spiritual Man,* Banner of Truth, 1972, p.75.
11. Boston, *Human Nature,* p.456.
12. As above, p.455.
13. *Works of John Owen,* vol. vii, p.339.
14. Gerstner, *Jonathan Edwards on Heaven and Hell,* pp.45-8.
15. Lloyd-Jones, *Studies in the Sermon on the Mount,* vol. i, p.113.
16. *Works of John Owen,* p.337.
17. Quoted in *Press Toward the Mark,* J. I. Packer, 'The Puritan Idea of Communion with God', Puritan and Reformed Studies Conference, 1962.
18. Boston, *Human Nature,* p.453.
19. Quoted by Lockyer in *The Gospel of the Life Beyond,* p.90.

Chapter 21 — A relief and Sabbath-rest
1. R. V. G. Tasker, *The Gospel according to Matthew,* Tyndale Press, 1961, p.121.
2. Calvin, *Christian Institutes II,* viii, p.29.

Chapter 23 — Heaven: our work there
1. W. Hendriksen, *More than Conquerors: an interpretation of the book of Revelation,* Tyndale Press (IVP), 1962, p.91.
2. The word is also used by other New Testament writers, as in 2 Peter 1:1; James 1:1; Jude 1, and as many as eight times in Revelation.
3. Iain H. Murray (ed.), *Diary of Kenneth Macrae,* Banner of Truth, 1980, p.506.

Chapter 24 — Heaven: we live there!
1. Spurgeon, *Metropolitan Tabernacle Pulpit,* vol. 37, p.533. The sermon is on 1 Timothy 6:12, 'Lay hold on eternal life,' and was preached on 19 March 1891.
2. Spurgeon, *Metropolitan Tabernacle Pulpit,* vol. 31/1885, Banner of Truth edition, 1971, p.548.
3. As above, p.549.

Chapter 25 — Heaven: a better country
1. Iain H. Murray, *D. Martyn Lloyd-Jones, The Fight of Faith, 1939-1981,* Banner of Truth, 1990, p.730.
2. As above, p.731.
3. As above, p.747.

Chapter 26 — Heaven: the new Jerusalem
1. Smith, *The Biblical Doctrine of Heaven,* p.239.
2. Ramm, *Them he Glorified,* p.106.
3. Derek Williams (ed.), *New Concise Bible Dictionary,* IVP and Lion Publishing, 1989, p.262.
4. See also Isaiah 48:2; 52:1-2; Nehemiah 11:1.

Notes 241

Chapter 27 — Heaven in relation to hell
1. See, for example, Edwards and Stott, *Essentials,* Hodder, 1988, pp.316-18.
2. In the Authorized and New King James Versions this statement appears as many as five times (vv. 43,44,45,46,48) so that the repetition is challenging.
3. Maurice Roberts, *The Thought of God,* Banner of Truth, 1993, p.219.
4. Quoted by Gerstner, *Jonathan Edwards on Heaven and Hell,* p.35.
5. As above, p.36.

Chapter 28 — Reaching heaven
1. Quoted by Elsie Houghton, *Christian Hymn-Writers,* Evangelical Press of Wales (now Bryntirion Press), 1982, p.29.
2. As above, p.69.
3. Carson, *The Gospel according to John,* p.290.

Chapter 29 — Reaching heaven: guaranteed for all Christians
1. D. Martyn Lloyd-Jones, *God the Father, God the Son,* Hodder & Stoughton, 1996, vol. i, pp.90-91.
2. Hodge, *The Confession of Faith,* p.232.
3. C. H. Spurgeon, 'For Whom Christ Died', *Banner of Truth* magazine, 5th issue, April 1957, pp.32-3.
4. John Bunyan, *Pilgrim's Progress,* Banner of Truth edition, 1977, p.29.

Chapter 30 — Heaven: living under its rule
1. *Concise Oxford Dictionary,* Ninth Edition, Oxford University Press, 1995, p.1020.
2. See, e.g. Romans 4:3-8; Ephesians 2:8-10.
3. George Whitefield, *Whitefield's Journals,* Banner of Truth, 1960, p.213.
4. As above, p.310.
5. Joni Eareckson Tada, *Heaven: What Will it be Like?* Marshall Pickering, 1995.
6. As above, p.58.
7. As above, p.59.

Chapter 31 — Heaven: crossing the river
1. Bunyan, *Pilgrim's Progress,* see pp.180-88.
2. Faith Cook, *Singing in the Fire,* Banner of Truth, 1995, p.60.
3. As above, pp.118-19.
4. As above, pp.118-20.
5. As above, p.146.
6. John Walters, *Storming the Golden Kingdom,* IVP, 1989, p.179.
7. Kuhn, *In the Arena,* p.228.
8. As above, p.229.
9. As above, p.232.
10. Faith Cook, *Grace in Winter: Rutherford in verse,* Banner of Truth, 1989, p.40.
11. Murray, *D. Martyn Lloyd-Jones: The Fight of Faith,* p.743.

Chapter 32 — Will I meet you in heaven?
1. J. Douglas MacMillan, *The God of All Grace,* Christian Focus Publications, 1997, pp.12-21.
2. Quoted by Lockyer, *The Gospel of the Life Beyond,* pp.100-101.

Appendix II — Heaven: are there rewards for Christians?
1. Berkhof, *Systematic Theology,* p.737.
2. Roberts, *The Thought of God,* p.227.
3. Oliphint & Ferguson, *Hoping for Heaven,* p.29.
4. Lockyer, *The Gospel of the Life Beyond,* p.79.
5. D. L. Moody, *Heaven ... and How to Get There,* Moody Press, undated, p.112.
6. Helm, *The Last Things,* p.104.
7. Bruce Milne, *Know the Truth,* IVP, 1982, p.273.
8. Quoted by Gerstner, *Jonathan Edwards on Heaven and Hell,* p.23.
9. Grudem, *Systematic Theology,* p.1144.
10. R. T. Kendall, *When God Says 'Well Done!',* Christian Focus Publications, 1993, p.929.
11. H. Z. Cleveland, *Evangelical Dictionary of Theology,* Marshall Pickering, 1985, p.952.
12. Helm, *The Last Things,* p.104.
13. As above, p.105.
14. Roberts, *The Thought of God,* p.227.
15. As above, p.226.
16. Milne, *Know the Truth,* p.273.
17. Berkhof, *Systematic Theology,* p.737.
18. Helm, *The Last Things,* p.105.
19. As above, p.106.
20. Grudem, *Systematic Theology,* p.1144.
21. Lockyer, *The Gospel of the Life Beyond,* pp.80-81.
22. As above, p.82.
23. Cleveland, *Evangelical Dictionary of Theology,* 'Reward', especially p.952.
24. Kendall, *When God Says 'Well Done!',* p.19.
25. As above, p.20.
26. As above, p.31.
27. As above, p.30.
28. Milne, *Know the Truth,* p.273.
29. Kendall, *When God Says 'Well Done!',* p.121.
30. Quoted by Craig Blomberg in 'Degrees of Reward in the Kingdom of Heaven', *Journal of the Evangelical Theological Society,* 35/2, p.162.
31. Leon Morris, *The Gospel according to Matthew,* IVP, 1992, p.137.
32. As above, p.138.
33. As above, p.139.
34. William Hendriksen, *The Gospel of Matthew,* Banner of Truth, 1974, p.321.
35. As above.
36. As above, p.479.
37. Morris, *The Gospel according to Matthew,* p.103.
38. Lloyd-Jones, *Studies in the Sermon of the Mount,* vol. 1, p.147.
39. For example, Hendriksen, *Matthew,* p.282.

40. Ralph Martin, *Philippians: an Introduction and Commentary,* IVP, 1959, p.165.
41. Hendriksen, *Epistle to the Philippians,* p.189.
42. Morris, *The Epistles of Paul to the Thessalonians,* p.59.
43. R. V. G. Tasker confirms this in *The General Epistle of James: an introduction and commentary,* Tyndale, IVP, 1956, p.45.
44. Douglas J. Moo in *The Letter of James,* Tyndale, IVP, 1985, pp.70-71. See also Alec Motyer in *The Message of James,* IVP, 1985, p.48.
45. See Wayne Grudem in *The First Epistle of Peter,* IVP, 1988, pp.190-91 and Alan M. Stibbs in *The First Epistle General of Peter,* Tyndale, IVP, 1959, p.168.
46. Philip Hughes, *The Book of the Revelation: a commentary,* IVP, 1990, p.61.
47. Hendriksen, *The Gospel of Matthew,* p.688.
48. David Gooding, *According to Luke: a new exposition of the third Gospel,* IVP, 1987, p.333.
49. William Hendriksen, *The Gospel of Luke,* Banner of Truth, 1978, p.972.
50. As above, p.972.
51. Morris, *The Gospel according to Matthew,* p.495.
52. Hendriksen, *The Gospel of Matthew,* p.730.
53. As above, p.731.
54. Donald A. Hagner, *Word Biblical Commentary: Matthew 14-28,* Word Books, Dallas, 1995, p.565.
55. R. T. Kendall, *Once Saved, Always Saved,* Ambassador, 1992, p.162.
56. Tasker, *The Gospel according to Matthew,* p.190.
57. Hagner, *Word Biblical Commentary,* p.572.
58. Craig L. Blomberg, 'Degrees of Reward in the Kingdom of Heaven', *Journal of the Evangelical Theological Society,* 35/2, p.160.
59. Morris, *The Gospel according to Matthew,* pp.617-18.
60. Hagner, *Word Biblical Commentary,* p.725.
61. E. Earle Ellis in, *New Century Bible Commentary: Luke,* Marshall, Morgan & Scott, 1981, p.222.
62. Bruce Milne, *Know the Truth,* IVP, 1982, p.273.
63. As above.
64. Hendriksen, *The Gospel of Luke,* p.863.
65. David Gooding, *According to Luke,* IVP, 1987, p.301.
66. Tasker, *The Gospel according to Matthew,* p.237.
67. Hendriksen, *The Gospel according to Matthew,* p.885.
68. Quoted by Morris in *The Gospel according to Matthew,* pp.633-4.
69. Gooding, *According to Luke,* p.246.
70. Ellis (*The New Century Bible Commentary: Luke,* p.181) is one writer who maintains the point and he may be correct.
71. Hendriksen, *The Gospel of Luke,* p.681; Gooding, *According to Luke,* p.246.
72. Kendall, *Once Saved, Always Saved* and *When God Says 'Well Done!'*
73. D. Carson, *The Cross and Christian Ministry: an exposition of passages from 1 Corinthians,* IVP, 1993, p.68.
74. Kendall, *When God Says 'Well Done!',* p.129.
75. Carson, *The Cross and Christian Ministry,* p.70.
76. As above.
77. Hodge, *The First Epistle to the Corinthians,* p.54.

78. Carson, *The Cross and Christian Ministry,* p.77.
79. Kendall, *When God Says 'Well Done!',* pp.32-3.
80. As above, p.61.
81. As above, pp.82-107.
82. As above, pp.103-5; see also pp.70-81.
83. Carson, *The Cross and Christian Ministry,* p.78.
84. See also 2:2.
85. Hodge, *The First Epistle to the Corinthians,* p.56.
86. Kendall, *When God Says 'Well Done!',* p.97.
87. Carson, *The Cross and Christian Ministry,* p.78.
88. Craig L. Blomberg in *Journal of the Evangelical Theological Society,* 35/2, June 1992, p.165. See also D. Prior, *The Message of 1 Corinthians,* IVP, 1985, p.60. Note also that because of the plural pronouns used and the context of verses 16-17, Gordon Fee underlines the corporate nature of the reward or its loss. The destruction becomes 'the church's failure to function any longer as a viable alternative to Corinth by manifesting the nature and fruit of the gospel within totally pagan surroundings', quoted by Blomberg, as above.
89. As above.
90. Kendall, *When God Says 'Well Done!',* p.85.
91. As above, p.98.
92. As above, p.105.
93. As above, pp.106-7.
94. Kendall, *Once Saved, Always Saved,* p.166.
95. As above.
96. As above, p.168; see also pp.183-4.
97. Kendall, *When God Says 'Well Done!',* p.103.
98. As above, p.104.
99. As above, pp.104-5.
100. As above, pp.138-9.
101. Ralph Martin. *40 Word Biblical Commentary: 2 Corinthians,* Word Publishing, 1991, p.114.
102. H. Moulton, *A Grammar of New Testament Greek,* T&T Clark, vol. iii: Syntax, 1963, p.72.
103. Martin, *40 Word Biblical Commentary,* p.114.
104. As above.
105. A. Plummer, *The International Critical Commentary: II Corinthians,* T & T Clark, 1915, pp.158-9.
106. Blomberg, *Journal of ETS,* 35/2, June 1992, p.165.
107. As above, p.160.

Index

Scripture index

Heaven is a far better place